The Flying BR

The Flying BR

THE HISTORY OF THE
NEW MEXICO
BOYS AND GIRLS RANCHES

ROBERT H. TERRY

SUNSTONE
PRESS

SANTA FE
NEW MEXICO

First edition

Printed in the United States of America

10 9 8 7 6 5 4 3 2 1

Library of Congress Catalog Card Number: 94-067002

ISBN: 0-86534-227-X

This book produced by: Sunstone Press
Post Office Box 2321
Santa Fe, New Mexico 87504-2321 / USA
(505) 988-4418 / FAX: (505) 988-1025

DEDICATION

*To Albert Buck
who dreamed the dream.*

*To Walker Hubbard
who kept the dream alive.*

*To the many, many
dedicated staff and friends.
Both past and present.
Who continue the dream
of giving youth
"The Right Chance."*

CONTENTS

ACKNOWLEDGMENTS

"Choose an author as you choose a friend."

So wrote the famous English writer, Wentworth Dillon, Earl of Roscommon, in the year 1684. This author will probably never know if Charles Gibson, former Executive Director of the Boys Ranch, knew of this verse or not when we first talked about this project.

Likewise, I did not know that by agreeing to put together the history of the Boys Ranch I would become an expert map reader, geographer, state-wide traveler, confidant, detective, admirer, and friend. Nor did I know that I would get to visit places like La Joya, Hurley, Veguita, Buckhorn, Carrizozo, and Melrose. Throw in our trips across Colorado and Texas, and this project has been a wonderful geographical safari.

More significant are the wonderful new friends that we have made along the way. The mention of "Boys Ranch" opened doors of hospitality with all of our interviewees. Now that I think about our treatment, it really was very biblical—"we were strangers and you took us in." Thank you.

A very special note of appreciation goes to Mike Kull, President of Boys and Girls Ranch, for without his aid and encouragement this project could not have been completed. Thanks also to Dr. Gerald May for his proof reading and comments. An additional note of appreciation goes to Bill and Martha Barrick of the Boys Ranch staff. They became our fountainhead of knowledge on subjects ranging from freeze drying fruit to how to select cactus wood.

At York College of Pennsylvania my appreciation goes to the Faculty Research Committee under Dr. Chin H. Suk and to Dr. Philip Avillo, Chairman of the Department of History and Political Science. Dr. Avillo has become an expert at designing my schedule to keep me writing. Appreciation also goes to my typist daughter, Paula, herself a teacher, and to Debbie White, a genius on the computer. Thanks also to Tim Taylor, critic, philosopher, and friend. Finally, a very special note of acknowledgment to my wife, Shirley, who made those many miles of travel across this big country of ours a whole lot more pleasant.

The mistakes, and given the nature of this project there are some, are mine alone. Reports, verbal and written, do not always agree. And people's recollections of past events sometime blur with the years. In any case, we have tried to set the record straight. Enjoy the story.

Robert H. Terry, Ph.D.
Dillsburg, Pennsylvania

INTRODUCTION

The Flying BR cattle brand was assigned to the first herd of cattle at the Boys Ranch and for years a sign bearing the same title directed visitors to the Ranch. Started by the Albuquerque Kiwanis Club as a civic response to juvenile delinquency, the leadership was provided by Albert Buck, the President of Rio Grande Steel and others. Soon some 2,600 acres of land was acquired along the Rio Grande River south of Belen, and the first building was constructed. Such was the demand for this type of facility that soon some sixty young boys crowded this one building under one set of houseparents.

Tragedy struck in 1951 with the sudden death of Al Buck and his wife in a flaming airplane crash. Financial crisis after crisis plagued the Ranch for years and threatened each time to close the Ranch. In 1954 Walker Hubbard, then considered the premier child care administrator in New Mexico, assumed the leadership of Boys Ranch. For eighteen years he divided his time between the Children's Home in Portales and the Boys Ranch serving as Superintendent of both.

Under the leadership of Walker Hubbard, Barry Morgan and others, the Ranch paid off its debts, stabilized the operation, and began to grow. When Mike Kull replaced Barry Morgan in 1972, the Ranch entered a new phase. Under Kull's leadership, and with twenty years of help from Charles Gibson, the Ranch matured to the point where it was ready to expand. That expansion exploded in the 1980s into the formation of the Girls Ranch, the Hart Youth Ranch, Families for Children and a Foundation. Thus as the Ranch prepared to celebrate its golden anniversary, it could look back in pride on all of its accomplishments. However, it may be that 1994 will prove to be the launching pad into the 21st Century. For it is the belief of the Ranch leadership that God has brought them through their years of trials and tribulation to prepare them for an even greater future. ■

Chapter One
THE BACKGROUND

New Mexico is called the "Land of Enchantment" and that it truly is, for the land forms, climate and people are remarkable in their diversity. It is a geographical fact that six of the world's known life zones exist within boundaries of the state's 121,412 square miles.

From the lofty pine covered slopes of Wheeler Peak (13,161 ft.) near Taos in the north, to the cactus-covered deserts of the south; from the llano estacado or staked plain in the east to the mesas of Navajo and Hopi country in the west the diversity is absolutely remarkable.

Add to the diversity the majesty of mountains like the Sangre de Cristo (Blood of Christ), the Manzanos, the Sacramentos, and the Guadalupes; include plants like the chamisa, yucca, sage, juniper, piñon, and cactus; toss in the Rio Grande River, top it all off with a deep turquoise sky and indeed New Mexico becomes someplace very special.

Some say that the magic is due to the clarity of the air; others say it is the low humidity and still others claim that it is due to the sun that shines virtually all year long. Whatever the case, trying to explain what is special about New Mexico to someone who has never been there is very difficult. Author Tony Hillerman may have best captured the essence of New Mexico in his book *The Spell of New Mexico* when he quotes Oliver LaFarge, that prolific Pulitzer Prize writer as saying:

It is a vast, harsh, poverty-stricken, varied, and beautiful land, a breeder of artists and warriors. It is the home, by birth or passionate adoption, of a wildly assorted population which has shown itself capable of achieving homogeneity without sacrificing its diversity. It is a land full of essence of peace, although its history is one of invasions and conflicts. It is itself, an entity, at times infuriating, at times utterly delightful to its lovers, a land that draws and holds men and women with ties that cannot be explained or submitted to reason.[1]

Not far from the modern city of Albuquerque is Sandia Cave, one of the earliest known archaeological sites in the entire southwest. It appears that man has been in the Rio Grande Valley since at least 12,000 B.C. Folsom Man, whose stone darts were uncovered near Raton and the occupants of Bat Cave who left remnants of domestic corn out in the Plains of San Agustin, were other prehistoric residents of New Mexico. Evidence of other early inhabitants can be gleaned from the numerous petroglyphs located in many parts of the state.

Pre-Colombian farmers (located mostly in the Northwest part of the state such as Chaco Canyon) created a highly developed religion, built impressive villages, worked extensively in pottery and weaving, and created sophisticated irrigation and road systems.[2] Today experts believe that these people traded as far away as Mexico and the Pacific Coast. However, by the time Francisco Vasquez de Coronado and his Spanish Conquistadors marched into the region in 1540, drought and hostile marauders had forced these early Native Americans into scattered pueblos (so named because they resembled Spanish towns).

In 1598 under the leadership of Don Juan de Onate the first permanent European settlers of New Mexico came north up the Rio Grande Valley. This thousand mile trip which took two years, brought ten Franciscan priests and one hundred twenty-nine soldiers—colonists and their families. When San Gabriel de los Españoles (near the present day site of the San Juan Pueblo north of Española) was the capital it was a thousand miles from any other European community. Hardship, lack of gold and silver, and finally large scale desertion forced the Spanish Empire to relocate down river to Santa Fe in 1610.

As the Spanish settlements in New Mexico (still part of New Spain) grew, the Franciscans worked harder to convert the locals to Christianity. For many this was the greatest insult of all and in 1680 the two cultures clashed. Known today as the Pueblo Revolt, a thousand frightened Spaniards retreated southward through the Valley all the way to El Paso, Texas. Some 2500 early colonists were killed in the struggle with priests frequently being singled out for brutal deaths.[3] Don Diego de Vargas (the rest of his name is Zapata y Lujan Ponce de Leon) who had kept the New Mexicans together in El Paso returned to Santa Fe on September 12, 1692, and received the Indian surrender without a shot being fired. Today the Spanish reconquest is celebrated, at least by the Hispanics and tourists, each fall in the Santa Fe Fiesta.

For 150 years, New Mexico served as the Northern-most outpost of Spain in the New World. In 1821 it became part of the Republic of Mexico. Linked only by the Camino Real (Chihuahua Trail) which ran 450 miles from Santa Fe down the Rio Grande Valley to Chihuahua, life was always difficult and "Mother Mexico" was far away. However, in spite of raids by the Apaches, Navajos, Utes and Comanches, the region grew.

New Mexico was opened to trade with the United States following Mexican independence. The link to the United States was called the Santa Fe Trail and by 1821 William Becknell had opened the trail all the way from Missouri. New Mexico was opened up to American trade, influence and settlement.

The city of Albuquerque lies on the banks of the Rio Grande and has developed over the years as the industrial and population hub of New Mexico. The Records of New Mexico's twenty-eighth colonial governor, Don Francisco Cuervo y Valdez, state that in the early part of 1706 the governor founded a villa which he named *San Francisco de Albuquerque*. This was in honor of Don Francisco Fernandez de la Cueva Enriquez, Duque de Albuquerque, the thirty-fourth Viceroy of New Spain, then resident in Mexico City.[4]

Governor Cuervo's letter to the Viceroy-Duke of Albuquerque dated April 24, 1706, states that he had found the villa on the margins and meadows of the Rio del Norte in a goodly place of fields, waters, pasturage, and timber. There were thirty-five families now living in the villa compromising 252 persons. Furthermore, a church had been built and other public buildings were being constructed. It is generally agreed that descendants of these founding families still live in the city.[5]

During the war with Mexico, General Stephen Kearney raised the American flag over the Palace of the Governors in Santa Fe in 1846, and New Mexico became a United States Territory. The action in Santa Fe was peaceful and without resistance. However, in Taos a Mexican uprising occurred the next year in which the territorial Governor Charles Bent was killed. Officially it was the Treaty of Guadalupe Hidalgo

signed in Mesilla (near Las Cruces) on February 2, 1848 which ended
the Mexican War and gave American title to New Mexico. In 1853
additional territory was added to both New Mexico and Arizona by the
Gadsden Purchase.

As historian Marc Simmons has noted, "The growth of the Santa Fe
trade and Kearney's conquest of 1846 marked the beginnings of The
Americanization of Albuquerque."[6] By 1860, the city could boast of a
population of some 1,760. During the civil war, Texas Confederates
moved up the Rio Grande Valley capturing both Albuquerque and Santa
Fe. The battle at Glorieta Pass, located between Santa Fe and Las Vegas, probably saved both the gold fields of Colorado and California for
the Union.

In the half century following The War Between the States, the
Territory of New Mexico truly lived up to the Eastern image of the "Wild
West." Indian wars were fought against the Apaches, Navajos, and Utes.
Kit Carson, the famous frontiersman from Taos served as the Indian
agent for eight years. In 1863 he brought six hundred Apaches to the
Bosque Redondo (near Ft. Sumner), and in 1864 he defeated the Navajos
at Canyon de Chelly and transferred seven thousand of them to the
Bosque. This plan did not work and in 1868 the Navajos were sent back
to their old territory in Northwestern New Mexico.

On Sunday, July 5, 1868 the residents of Albuquerque were treated
to a historic sight as the first of 7,000 Navajo, 100 military supply
wagons, and 6,000 head of livestock began their passage through the city
towards home.

> Twenty-one days after leaving the reservation, the column
> reached the mouth of Tijeras Canyon. The Indians in the lead
> gazed out across East Mesa, now greened by unusually
> abundant spring rains, and they saw the spires of San Felipi
> Neri Church lifting above the distant line of Albuquerque's
> roof tops. But what stirred them to their moccasin soles was
> the sharp, sparkling outline on the far horizon of their sacred
> mountains, Tso Dzil, the white man's Mount Taylor, home of
> the Navajo deities Turquoise Boy and Yellow Corn Girl. At
> the sight of that holy place, still 70 miles away, people wept
> openly and one man became temporarily deranged and had
> to be tied to a wagon gate by the soldiers until he regained his

senses. Recalling that moment long after an aged Navajo said: "When we saw the top of the mountain from Albuquerque . . . We felt like talking to the ground, we loved it so."[7]

Other events of the period have left their marks on New Mexico as well. Apaches fled the Bosque and took to the warpath and the famous chief Geronimo quit fighting in 1886. Range wars erupted across the state with the most famous being the Colfax County War in the northeast and the Lincoln County War in the south. William Bonney, alias Billy the Kid, became a sort of New Mexico celebrity as the result of these struggles.

However, the recorded natural disasters that fell on the territory were far worse than anything that man could do. For example, in 1865, late heavy frosts hit the upper Rio Grande Valley, then came torrential rains followed by hail. Flooding in Bernalillo County swept away the wheat and corn as the population of Albuquerque fled to the hills. A plague of grasshoppers descended and devoured everything that was left. The Valley, usually a producer of extra crops, harvested almost nothing. The Santa Fe Gazette put the misery this way: "Properly to describe the misery created by frost, flood and other combinations of earth and sky this year, a man ought to write with tears instead of ink."[8]

New Mexican historian Marc Simmons pays tribute to those early residents of the city when he says:

> . . . but in a day when catastrophes were as common as needles on a piñon tree, inhabitants along the Rio Grande had learned to bounce back. Albuquerque, though more than a century and a half old, was still a frontier town in spirit, and its people, being of the pioneering breed knew how to shrug off losses and build and plant again.[9]

Mining hit New Mexico in the 1870s and boom towns opened all over the state. Gold, silver, copper, lead, zinc, and turquoise boomed and busted leaving the state dotted with ghost towns.[10]

With mining came the railroads and New Mexico's relationship with various railroads is a story unto itself and not to be told here. However, in 1879, the Atchison, Topeka and Santa Fe were granted a charter to operate in the Territory. The subsidiary of the ATSF formed to handle the New Mexican routes was to be called the New Mexico and Southern Pacific Railroad Company and as the saying goes, "the race was on."

As with many of these railroads in this time period, the Santa Fe was building track faster than it could raise capital. The profits were to be in the future but for the present, budgets were tight. Failure to understand this economic phenomenon cost several New Mexican towns their future. A case in point is Las Vegas whose failure to grant the railroad its demands (money, land, etc.) cost them their business district as the line was built a mile away. The Territorial capital actually fared the worse for the town fathers turned down the money requests from not one but two railroads. They then watched in horror as the Denver and Rio Grande stopped at Española twenty miles to the north and the Santa Fe passed the capital to the south through Lamy.[11]

Credit the early leaders of Albuquerque with foresight and tenacity for the last rails were laid into the city by 4:00 p.m. on April 5, 1880, and on April 22nd the city went wild with official celebration. Albuquerque was being hailed as the "Queen City of the Rio Grande" and the "Chicago of the West."[12]

The New Albuquerque was established in 1880 a mile and a half east of the Old Town Plaza. When company officials back in Boston and Kansas decided to make Albuquerque the site for the division point between Kansas and California, the city's future was assured. By locating the Santa Fe's largest locomotive repair shops in the New Albuquerque, the local economy was given an industrial base. Soon New Mexico's largest urban center numbered some 6,335 inhabitants, over 85 percent of whom were "Anglo."[13]

Charles D. Biebel has observed that: "For a generation, newcomers strove to reproduce the economic patterns, architectural styles, and cultural institutions familiar to eastern Victorian society."[14] His Museum of Albuquerque publication goes on to paint the following picture:

> The foundation of New Albuquerque was the Santa Fe Railroad. In addition to providing a means of immigration for the new population, railroad offices, repair shops, and daily trains introduced wage labor—a twelve hour industrial workday and the regularity of a six day industrial work week—into a largely no-cash traditional agricultural society. The scream of the locomotive and the blast of shop whistles now punc-

tuated the older natural rhythms of farming seasons.[15]

The Santa Fe Railroad dominated Albuquerque well into the twentieth century. Foundries and machine shops stood along side railroad repair shops. Sheep, cattle, wool, hides, railroad ties and lumber moved eastward out of Albuquerque. Culturally the Santa Fe offered a cheap and rapid way west from the East and the Midwest. Although the local population increased dramatically after 1890, the new citizens were overwhelmingly native born or "old European" foreign born. Over half of the foreign born immigrants came from northern Europe or Canada (Great Britain, Germany, Canada and Scandinavia in that order). In 1920 native-born Hispanos comprised more than 25 percent of the local population.[16]

Historians usually agree that the most outstanding character of national life at the turn into the twentieth century was the rise of the cities. Albuquerque was soon to become one of those cities. Albuquerque historian E.P. Harrington is quoted as saying, "Never forget that practically every decade since 1880 has been a boom decade in this town."[17]

Shortly after the turn of the century, Albuquerque and all of New Mexico were being acclaimed as a health seekers paradise. As one journalist gushed, "Albuquerque is one of the cities of the West that is so openly, so rampantly healthy, so gloriously deluged with vivifying sunshine and purified and healing breezes that it invites with open arms the sick and ailing to enter its portals."[18] Attention became world wide when a French medical society issued a statement asserting that, of all the habitable places in the world, New Mexico was the area most free of consumption, as tuberculosis was then called.[19] This was no small claim when one considers that tuberculosis was at that time the chief cause of death in the United States.

By 1910 Albuquerque boasted three major hospitals and by the end of World War I, five more private sanatoriums had been established. This was not just a direct economic benefit to the city, but many of those who recovered stayed on in New Mexico and made valuable contributions to the city and state. Perhaps the most famous of these "lungers," as tuberculosis patients were called, was Clinton Anderson who started as a city newspaper man and then went on to become a United States Senator.

During the 1920s Albuquerque continued to boom both through private enterprise and through municipal government and state agencies. The new courthouse was dedicated in May of 1926 and dominated the north end of the central business district. The decorative KiMo Theater built in 1927 is probably the last impressive commercial monument to this boom era. During the 1920s Albuquerque became the first city in New Mexico to pass the 10,000 population figure.[20]

In 1929, one year after Albuquerque's first radio station, KGGM went on the air, the stock market crashed. While the Great Depression had its worst effects in the East, the economic crisis soon hit the entire west. Banks closed, businesses failed, and lines of the unemployed were soon seen on the streets. While vacationers stopped coming, the city streets were soon filled with the hungry and desperate fleeing the Dust Bowl and Depression. Many families simply passed through the city on their way to California.

John Steinbeck immortalized old Route 66, now Central Avenue, with his epic book *The Grapes of Wrath*. Historian Marc Simmons says:

> Albuquerque retail and whole sale firms suffered their own woes. Contraction of the Markets forced many to seek loans to stave off bankruptcy, but rarely was money available. Farmers and ranchers in outlying areas made stringent cutbacks in the amount of supplies purchased in the city as their incomes plummeted alarmingly. After 1931, bankers virtually ceased making loans to cattlemen.[21]

By 1933 business in Albuquerque was at a standstill. The belt-tightening hit the city schools very hard and it was estimated that some 8,000 school children state wide were not receiving any education because their schools had closed.

Albuquerque's colorful mayor, Clyde Tingley, helped to funnel in numerous federal projects through the Works Progress Administration (WPA) and the Civilian Conservation Corps (CCC). Projects included parks, a railroad overpass at Central Avenue, The Little Theater, a zoo, an airport terminal, buildings for the state fair (which opened in 1938), and a wall (later removed) around the Old Town Plaza. The largest WPA projects were at the University of New Mexico and totalled more than $1,000,000. Both the Lobo Stadium and Zimmerman Library were built at this time. Remarkable as it seems, the University experienced a 600% increase in enrollment during the Depression.[22]

It is extremely interesting to note that Albuquerque and most of New Mexico came out of the Depression with a general feeling of optimism. Symbolic evidence of this attitude was displayed by native son Conrad Hilton who built his new ten story Hilton Hotel in 1939. Yet in all probability it was the completion of this new Albuquerque in August 1939 that symbolized the coming of the city's greatest boom.

Due to one of the largest airport runways in the United States and the excellent flying weather, the United States Army Air Corps in 1940 designated the city as a base for its military planes. By 1942 the base was called Kirtland Field and was used to train crews for the B-17s known as Flying Fortresses.

The military found the desert south of Albuquerque to be a perfect testing ground for all sorts of weapons including bombing ranges, aerial gunnery, and ultimately the atomic bomb. Meanwhile, northwest of Santa Fe on the lonely Pajarito Plateau, Robert J. Oppenheimer and his scientific colleagues were creating the secret Los Alamos Laboratories.

The famous Manhattan Project came to fruition on July 16, 1945 when the shockwave of the world's first atomic bomb swept out from the Trinity Site. Across the state, houses rattled and as far away as Gallup windows blew out. Author Lansing Lamont in his book *The Day of Trinity* says, "The Pyrotechnic display, visible for hundreds of miles, resembled nothing less than the fires of Hell."[23]

One thing was for sure, New Mexico was entering a new era. The thousands of servicemen, scientists, government employees, and job seekers of all types were dramatically changing the face of Central New Mexico, especially the city of Albuquerque. In 1940 the city counted a population of about 35,000. Increasing by some 500 percent, this population reached 175,000 by 1955. As author Marc Simmons notes, "In the process, the casual Western lifestyle, a holdover from the nineteenth century, began to be replaced by the high pressure living typical of modern urban America."[24]

In its preface, The Albuquerque Museum History Monograph titled *Making the Most Of It* has captured the essence of the times perfectly when saying:

. . . There was a profound transformation of the prevailing

social, political, and economic conditions. To many it appeared
as if Albuquerque's destiny was being determined by powerful
men and bureaucratic agencies in Washington, D.C. While
there was some truth to this perception, numerous local men
and women were acting decisively on their own ideas and
values to shape the future of the city.[25]

One of those men of vision was named Albert E. Buck!

NOTES:

1.   Oliver LaFarge from the Estate of Oliver LaFarge 1952, and
     quoted in *The Spell of New Mexico*, Tony Hillerman, Editor.
     University of New Mexico Press, Albuquerque, 1976.
2.   *The Anasazi*, J. Richard Ambler Museum of Northern Arizona,
     Flagstaff, AZ, 1977.
3.   Franklin Folson, *Red Power on the Rio Grande* (Chicago: Follett
     Publishing Com., 1973.)
4.   *New Mexico Place Names: A Geographical Dictionary*. Edited by T.M.
     Pearce, University of New Mexico Press. 1983. pages 5 and 6.
5.   Ibid.
6.   *Albuquerque: A Narrative History.* Marc Simmons. University
     of New Mexico. 1982. p. 142.
7.   Simmons op cit, p. 194.
8.   Simmons.
9.   Simmons op cit, p. 195.
10. Author's Note: One example of a ghost town is that of Blossburg
     in Colfax County near Raton. Settled in 1881 as a coal mining
     town by a Colonel Savage from Blossburg, PA, which incidentally
     is the home of both sets of the author's grandparents. It was
     named for Savage's hometown and had its own post office from
     1881 to 1905. Today, there is little left at this site. Other more
     famous ghost towns such as Elizabethtown, Golden and Piños
     Altos dot the New Mexican landscape.
11. For fascinating reading on the Denver and Rio Grande Railroad—
     Chile Line: The Narrow Rail Trail to Santa Fe by John A. Gjeore 1969.
     Rio Grande Sun Press Española, New Mexico.
12. Simmons op cit, p. 214.
13. Simmons, op cit, quoted in *Making the Most Of It: Public Works*

in Albuquerque during the Great Depression 1929-1942 Charles D. Biebel, the Albuquerque Museum, 1986, p. 1.

14. *Public Works in Albuquerque,* op cit, p. 1.
15. *Public Works in Albuquerque,* op cit, p. 1.
16. Fourteenth Census of the U.S., "Population, 1920" (Washington, D.C. Government Printing Office, 1920), p. 670-672 quoted in *Public Works in Albuquerque* op cit.
17. Biebel, op cit. preface.
18. Max Frost *New Mexico Bureau of Immigration* Santa Fe, New Mexico, 1894. p. 274. Quoted in Simmons, op cit, p. 343.
19. Ibid.
20. Oppenheimer, *Historical Background of Albuquerque,* p. 42.
21. Simmons, op cit, p. 359.
22. Simmons, op cit, p. 365.
23. Lansing Lamont. *The Day of Trinity.* N.Y. Athenaeum. 1965. p. 53.
24. Simmons, op cit, p. 366.
25. *Making the Most Of It: Public Works in Albuquerque During the Great Depression 1929-1942.* Charles D. Biebel. An Albuquerque Museum History Monograph 1985.

Chapter Two
THE BEGINNING

On D-Day June 6, 1944 thousands of Allied troops stormed the beaches of Normandy in France. In the Pacific American troops returned to the Philippines, and in Washington, D.C. at a place called Dumbarton Oaks the future of the United Nations was finally agreed upon. Meanwhile, half a continent away in Albuquerque, New Mexico juvenile delinquency was rapidly becoming a problem. As a response to this growing problem one service club, the Albuquerque Kiwanis Club, organized a Boys Rehabilitation Committee. Among those club members who became deeply concerned were Al Buck, Cecil Pragnell and Judge Albert R. Kool. An open discussion meeting among all the Kiwanis led to the thought of Father Flanagan and his famous "Boys Town" in Nebraska. Thus was born the concept of New Mexico Boys Ranch.

During the first six months of 1944 discussions were held and a general working outline of Ranch objectives was decided upon. These included:

1. An age limit of 7 to 14
2. Boys only (not girls at this time)
3. All races would be welcomed
4. The Ranch was to be non-political
5. The Ranch was to be interdenominational

Prior to the actual admission a Board would pass judgement on the moral and physical fitness of each and every boy. Each boy would become a ward of the New Mexico Boys Ranch until such time they could be released to a parent or guardian.

Al Buck, who gave so generously of his time, money and energy knew in his heart, as did the men behind him, that if a young boy was just given "the right chance" he could grow up to become a good, solid citizen. The earliest Ranch documents reveals the following: "The incorporation of the New Mexico Boys Ranch, a corporation not for profit, held their first meeting at the Chamber of Commerce building in the city of Albuquerque, New Mexico, on the 26th day of September 1944, at 7:30 o'clock p.m."[1]

According to these documents the founding fathers are as follows: Albert E. Buck, O.E. Beck, Carl Brogan, Cecil Pragnell, R.P. Woodson, Jr., Sid Murray, George L. Tucker, J.G. Ruvolo, and Charles Minton.

Chairman Buck announced to this gathered group of men that the *Certificate of Incorporation* had been filed with the State Corporation Commission on the 20th day of September, 1944 and a copy was also filed with the county clerk of Bernalillo County, New Mexico, on the 25th day of September, 1944. This same meeting saw officers and a Board of Directors elected as follows:

> President   - Albert E. Buck
> Vice-President - Carl Brogan
> Secretary   - Charles L. Minton
> Treasurer   - Sid Murray

These four men plus George L. Tucker, J.G. Ruvolo and O.E. Beck made up the first Board of Directors.

Minutes of this meeting indicate that Charles Minton was appointed as the first Director of Admissions and that a Board of Advisors was elected as follows: A.M. Markham, Homer Lawrence, Judge Albert R. Kool, Walter A. Biddle, R.P. Woodson, Jr., and Cecil Pragnell. By a unanimous vote of those present, the insignia of the corporation was adopted and is described as: the Zia sun symbol, color yellow orange, with the Flying BR brand mark in black in the center of the symbol and the words "New Mexico Boys Ranch" in black around the circumference of the symbol. The Flying BR brand was then registered with the State Cattle Sanitary Board as the official cattle brand of the Ranch.

Membership of this first board was composed entirely of men. However, it is interesting to note that according to the minutes new membership applications with checks for twelve and ten dollars were received from Katherine M.M. Woodson (R.P. Woodson's wife) and Florence O. McMillen (relationship unknown).

An examination of the Certificate of Incorporation spells out very explicitly the exact purpose of the New Mexico Boys Ranch when it states:

The object and purpose of this corporation shall be rehabilitation, education, and vocational training of underprivileged
boys and to serve *in loco parentis* to such boys as may be
accepted by the Board of Directors. The directors shall be the
sole exclusive judges of who shall be dismissed or expelled.
Upon the expulsion of any boy, the directors shall notify the
parents or guardians of such boy, if that is feasible, or the
appropriate public official is charged with the care of juvenile
delinquency matters, and thereupon the corporation and its
officials shall be under no further obligation or duty to such
expelled boy.[2]

At the October 3rd meeting "Those present voted unanimously to
have the membership cards contain the word `Buckaroo' instead of
member, in order to create more of a ranch atmosphere."[3] During this
meeting discussions were held on the Boys Ranch located near Dallas,
Texas to serve as a possible model. A lengthy discussion also occurred
on the site possibilities for the new ranch. The decision was made to
present the new Boys Ranch program to the Kiwanis District Convention
to be held in Arizona and to ask for support for it in eastern Arizona.
Records do not indicate whether any such help came but obviously
through Al Buck and others the Kiwanis Clubs of New Mexico played a
very important role, especially during these early years.[4]

Two weeks later in a meeting held at the County House, the First
National Bank in Albuquerque gave their authorization for President
Buck and Treasurer Murray to co-sign all checks for the organization.
Reports made at this meeting indicate that presentations about the
future Ranch were made to the Women's Club, the 20-30 Club of
Albuquerque and business cards were handed out at Optimist meetings
in El Paso, Texas.

At this same meeting there continued to be considerable discussion
about sites for the Boys Ranch. It was generally agreed that Board
members would talk to the Reconstruction Finance Corporation regarding land in the Middle Rio Grande Conservancy District, the Santa Fe
Railway land office, The Soil Conservation Service, and the U.S. Forest
Service and Grazing Service. The search for the best possible price was
on! The official new letterhead of the Boys Ranch, designed by Walter

Raabe of Albuquerque, was approved. Director R.P. Woodson exhibited a calendar with useful information for ranchers which would be imprinted with the name of *The New Mexico Boys Ranch* and distributed throughout the state at his own expense.[5]

On October 31, 1944, President Al Buck reported to the Board on his interviews with Judge Coors concerning a site for the Boys Ranch, saying that the Judge was very much interested in the program and would make efforts to see whether there was a site available within the Middle Rio Conservancy District. This is probably how the Ranch Board learned about the site that was eventually selected.[6] Other sites being offered or considered were the E.L. Young property in Belen which was thought to be too expensive and the Sweet Ranch near Cerrillos. The latter site was termed a good location although the elevation of 6,600 feet was too high and the question of water rights would require further investigation.

President Buck announced that he, Judge Kool, Mr. Ruvolo and Mr. Minton were scheduled for a statewide radio broadcast over station KOB on November 8th to publicize the Ranch. With the advisors joining in, a discussion was held on the educational phase of the Boys Ranch. An item of historical interest was the discussion concerning the use of the Ranch for veterans of World War II with medical discharges who needed rehabilitation. Apparently nothing ever materialized regarding these veterans.[7]

Cecil Pragnell, one of the original board members and years later an actual ranch manager, reported to the November gathering that as Chairman of the Site Committee, he and Mr. Minton (the first secretary) had inspected sites at Los Lunas (The Marshall Sellman's Ranch) and a site just south of Albuquerque (The Alvis Denison's Ranch), but that neither were entirely acceptable due to the fact that they were too close to the City of Albuquerque. Obviously, the original idea of getting the boys away from the city was still clear in the minds of the directors.

During the last meeting of the first year held at the County Court House on December 9, 1944, the secretary reported that two sites were available in the vicinity of Carlsbad. There were also reports of presentations on behalf of the Boys Ranch having been made to the Alamogordo Rotary Club, The Roswell Lions Club, and the Carlsbad Elks Lodge. The last order of business was the instructions to the secretary to take the necessary steps to obtain authorization from the

Bureau of Internal Revenue exempting donations to the Boys Ranch for income tax purposes.[8]

During two meetings in March of 1945 considerable discussion was held on the proposal to purchase the Black Ranch located at Alameda some eight-and-a-half miles north of Albuquerque in Bernalillo County. This was apparently a serious consideration for at one of the meetings A.F. Black, the owner, was present and presented a ranch survey of the 2,000 acres. From a reading of the records one gets the picture of a ranch with forty head of dairy cattle (worth, in those days, $25 each), a site divided by two roads, and about 375 acres that would have to be leveled at an estimated cost of $100 per acre. The Board agreed that the future Boys Ranch would be "beef" rather than "dairy" cattle and A.F. Black's proposal was rejected. The March 12, 1945 minutes list a Treasurer's report showing a total of $2,571.66.[9]

During the April 6th meeting, a new proposal was made for a ranch site at San Ysidro, forty-seven miles Northwest of Albuquerque. At this meeting first mention is made of the Chadwick property in Socorro County which embraced some 2,000 acres with 160 acres being under cultivation, and 1,200 acres of range. The asking price was $25,000. A careful reading of the geographic description can leave no doubt but that this would be the site of the future Boys Ranch. This property contained two wells near a small two-room adobe dwelling, described as the only building on the property.

Astute businessmen that they were, these early "founding fathers" met with officials of the Middle Rio Grande Conservancy District and consulted their maps of the property. It appears that at this time, a Mr. Lescallet informed the committee that delinquent conservancy assessments of five dollars per acre for the past ten years were due. According to his figures, the total would be approximately $34,200. He also reported to them that title to the property had reverted to the State of New Mexico in 1939, due to non-payment of taxes, and that the title was now in the state's hands.[10] In the same report Pragnell offered his opinion that the state would forgive half of all taxes, except current levies, which would have to be paid in full. Pragnell also said that the Conservancy District could not forgive any of the past due assessments on the property.[11]

On April 20th Secretary Minton met with Cal Farley, of the well-known Texas Boys Ranch near Amarillo, seeking his opinion on the site selection. Mr. Farley urged the group to start at the earliest possible moment on whatever site was available.

At a meeting in the famous Alvarado Hotel on May 7, 1945 on a motion by Charles Minton and seconded by Cecil Pragnell it was unanimously agreed upon to file a Third Party bid with the state for title to this ranch property.[12] While the specific amounts of back taxes are never mentioned it was generally agreed to offer to pay fifty percent of them.

The October 1945 meeting must have been a very busy one for the list of "Things to Do While Waiting" (meaning waiting for the title of the ranch) included: asking the Army about Salvage beds and furnishings, investigating the neighborhood school, contracting farmers and ranchers for stock and poultry, asking a woman to head the drive among women's organizations, investigate the procurement of farm tools and equipment, selecting a slogan for the campaign, getting a Fund Chairman, broadcasting the qualifications for a director and wife, preparing radio scripts for radio stations in New Mexico and Texas, etc. The list goes on and on and behind most items is the name of the man who was to complete the task.

An interesting comment on those times as well as on the remote location of the ranch site is found in the fact that the Albuquerque Kiwanis Boys and Girls Committee gave a gift of $100 for a "home radio." Records indicate that there were no phones in the vicinity of the Ranch. As fate would have it two of the most popular songs in the country that year were "Accentuate the Positive" and "Don't Fence Me In" both of which were highly appropriate.

The highlight of the November meeting was the hiring of Gordon Ferguson, an Albuquerque architect, to draw up the architectural sketches for the Ranch. Ferguson completed his plan within a year and donated his bill of $750 to the Ranch. President Al Buck reported that a Tax Deed free of objectionable conditions and provisions had been received from the State Tax Commission and that the same had been filed for record and duly recorded in Book 144, Pages 327-328 of Records of Deeds in the County of Socorro, New Mexico, at two o'clock p.m. on October 2, 1945.[13]

During November Colonel George W. Lewis was engaged by the

Board to assume responsibility for conducting the first financial campaign. By the end of the year the Colonel announced that approximately $6,100 had been received, with over one thousand separate contributions being counted.

In an interesting story of local political and military maneuvering Colonel Lewis called on a certain Colonel Harper, then Commandant at Kirtland Field, and requested an aerial photograph of the Ranch site. Receiving no response to mere civilians on the Board the good Colonel then gave proof that it was really the Hugh A. Carlisle Post Number 13 of the American Legion which had requested such a photograph. Colonel Harper then got the necessary authorization from Washington and two prints of the requested photo were received. Unfortunately, those early photographs can no longer be located. Thus ended the first full year of activity concerning the Boys Ranch.

By January of 1946, Colonel Lewis reported that the fund raising drive had reached $17,426.96. As was to be the case in the future the Boys Ranch organization drew a very special line concerning what was and what was not considered proper fund raising activities. Thus when the Albuquerque Heights Lions Club raffled off a Ford sold at cost to them by the Joe Heaston Motor Company it was the Lions, not the Ranch that conducted this activity. The next month when a boxing match was promoted by the Barelas Community Center, and sanctioned by Dr. Joaquin Ortega, the full support of the organization was given. Dr. Ortega, a respected Albuquerque educator along with Manuel Otero and Max R. Salazar became the first Hispanics to join the Board of Directors and Advisors.

From the minutes of the First Annual Meeting held at the Chamber of Commerce Building on January 28, 1946 comes some interesting comments on the religious consideration being planned for the boys. Father George V. Rieffer, representing Roman Catholic Archbishop Byrne, appeared at the meeting to clarify future religious training. After a thorough discussion Father Rieffer announced his satisfaction and said he would report favorable to the Archbishop.

The Board then divided itself into the following standing committees: Grounds and Buildings, Ranch Management, Education and Recreation, Membership and Coordination, Furnishings and Equipment, Finance, and Health and Hygiene. While the majority of committee members were from Albuquerque others were from Las Vegas, Clayton, Clovis, Roswell, and State College (Las Cruces today). Also included were Clarence Henderson, the Conservationist in Socorro County, and Mrs. Mary Watson, the State Supervisor of Elementary Education.

The Treasurer's report for January 28, 1946 is the first printed report available today. It shows a balance of $14,314.65 in the First National Bank and $1,000 deposited in the Albuquerque National Bank.[14] Board members traveled the state soliciting support. Mr. Ruvolo made trips to Springer, Raton, Roy, Las Vegas, Clovis, and Portales. While Colonel Lewis proceeded to organize a general committee for support in Dona Ana County.

At the February 19th meeting held at the El Fidel Hotel in Albuquerque, the Membership and Coordination Committee, now called the Personnel Committee, chaired by Charles Minton and composed of Judge Kool, Cecil Pragnell, R.P. Woodson, and A.M. Markham recommended the hiring of the first Ranch "Father and Mother" who were Mr. & Mrs. Andrew Gordon. Their employment was to begin on March 18, 1946 at a salary of $331.50 and Gordon was allowed six cents per mile on the use of his own car on Ranch business. When housing was completed at the Ranch, Mrs. Gordon was to be hired with the combined salary to be $350 per month, with housing, food, and utilities furnished.[15]

The first actual work at the new Ranch was reported by Mr. Gordon in late March. At that time he stated that water was found by the well drillers at 102 feet. He recommended that efforts be made to obtain fence posts and barbed wire and that adobes be ordered. He also recommended that arrangements be made to hire machinery, equipment, and labor necessary to do the spring plowing.

The question of housing for the boys was discussed with a letter from U.S. Senator Hatch being read to the group. The Senator suggested that the Flying BR as the Ranch was being called, contact nearby air bases (meaning Kirtland and Carlsbad) to see if any housing could be utilized. Carl Brogan was appointed to meet with Tom Popejoy at the University to see if he knew of any suitable military housing.

Throughout the Spring of 1946 board members and advisors continued to spread word of the Boys Ranch plan. Dr. Ortega and Mr. Ruvolo spoke to the first conference of the New Mexico Health Planning Council. Dr. Ortega solicited support from the Congress of Parents and

Teachers at its state convention in Las Cruces. Mr. Minton addressed the Roswell Convention of New Mexico Federation of Women's Clubs and the District Convention of Optimists with both groups promising substantial support. By June the State Convention of the Knights of Columbus, the New Mexico Osteopathic Association, and the New Mexico Dental Society had all endorsed the Boys Ranch program.

At the May 13, 1946 meeting Andrew Gordon, the first Ranch Manager, reported part of the 130 acres plowed had been planted, 15,000 adobes and 50,000 "terrones bricks" were made, and work on a variety of other items had begun. (See Story One.) The President commended Gordon warmly for his exceptional and dedicated services, saying, "that he deserved the thanks of the corporation for extraordinarily fine work."[16]

The Boys Ranch was growing and the work load on board members was increasing. Informal discussions were held on the need for a statewide organization which would be operated by a full-time business manager who would work closely with Gordon. These informal discussions turned into a Special Committee which recommended the employment of an Executive Director but no salary was ever mentioned. At the same meeting the new Executive Director was authorized to sign all checks and drafts. This may be the root of the first personnel problem at the Ranch.

By July the Executive Board, at the request of Gordon, defined his status and his duties. His title was made that of "Ranch Manager." Very specific details were agreed upon by the Executive Board including the transportation, the reception of the boys, and their religious services.

Throughout the summer, plans were made for more construction in addition to the four-room house for the Gordons. Unfortunately, the bank balance of approximately $10,000 did not merit more buildings. One of the more interesting proposals of that summer came from Tom Snell, Secretary of the New Mexico Sheep Sanitary Board, who brought forward a plan to run sheep at the Flying BR. This plan was ultimately rejected due to the lack of "wolf-proof" fencing.

September started off on a nice note with R.P. Woodson distributing the "1947" Boys Ranch calendars. Some 500 were printed at his own expense. During the same month his wife had set up a booth at the State Fair in which several Albuquerque women answered questions about the Boys Ranch. Also O.E. Beck and the Llewellyn Sign Co. offered to erect a large descriptive sign board at the junction of U.S. 85 and U.S. 60. It was at this September meeting that the first Ranch animals were pledged. A certain Mr. Lee gave five pigs and a Jersey milk cow, and Al Mitchell gave five yearlings, six two-year old heifers, and a bull.

It was obvious, by this time that the Executive Board was concerned over the "lack of coordinated effort due to the lack of a single channel of authority."[17] The Board tried to determine why Gordon could not work with the new Executive Director, Charles Minton. After a closed meeting on September 12, 1946 President Buck announced that all instructions from the Board would be channelled through the Executive Director. This was followed by a blistering letter to Gordon from Al Buck which concluded by stating: "It would be better not to move into the house until this matter is settled once and for all and to everyone's entire satisfaction."[18] From an historical perspective what is also interesting about this letter is that it was on the letterhead stationary of the Rio Grande Steel Products Company (Al Buck's company) and maybe the only letter in the Ranch files with this letterhead.

Apparently the relationship between Minton and Gordon did not improve and at the same time the financial conditions worsened. The October 17th financial statement showed a balance in all accounts of only $3,044.07 including $2,000 which had been loaned to the Corporation by Al Buck. The Board then informed the Gordons that the financial statement made it necessary for their salary to be reduced from $350 per month to $250 (a $100 per month reduction). It also informed Mrs. Gordon that she was to be the full-time cook, etc.[19] When the Gordons replied that they would accept the pay cut providing that "there be no remote control, interference, or any consumption of time on the part of the Executive Director." The Board blew a fuse and considered this letter to be their resignation. The Gordons left the Ranch on November 10, 1946 thus ending the short-lived career of the first Ranch Manager. In departing, the Gordons placed claims for $600 for Mrs. Gordon and $158.34 for broken/lost tools for Mr. Gordon. These claims were settled in full by action at the December Board Meeting.

Personality conflict, conflicting goals, unclear responsibilities—who can say for sure today what the problems really were. In retrospect it is fascinating to read Mrs. (Deweylee) Gordon's obituary which appeared in the Albuquerque Journal on February 2, 1990. She was 88 when she died, having come to New Mexico in 1908 by covered wagon from Oklahoma. Her family were homesteaders near San Jon in Quay County, which really got the attention of this author who lives in Dillsburg, Pennsylvania birthplace of Senator Matthew Quay for whom the county is named. San Jon boomed when the railroad came through in 1904 and Mrs. Gordon's family must have been among the earliest newcomers. She was a well-educated woman having attended Oklahoma State Teachers College (now OSU), the University of Oklahoma, Texas Tech and the University of New Mexico. She taught school in Oklahoma, Colorado, and New Mexico.

Perhaps the most interesting statement in her obituary is the statement that "she and her husband purchased the land for the Boys Ranch of New Mexico, which was founded in 1944." Did the Gordons actually sign the papers? Were they the people who handled the money? The official documents mention nothing. However, Shorty Ulibarri (see Story One) recalls Mr. Gordon as "the man who bought a big tract of land." Will we ever know? The Gordons had two small boys with them during 1946, which must have been difficult all the way around. These boys were Ladd, who became a director of the New Mexico State Department of Game and Fish, and his brother Larry, who was a secretary of the State Department of Health and Environment. Obviously someone did something correct in raising these children.[20]

In the minutes of the Committee of Admission of November and December appear the list of actual names of boys being admitted to the new Ranch. Names listed included: John (address unlisted), Earl (address unlisted), Jackie (Belen), Lee (Carlsbad), Russell (address unlisted), and Billy Wayne (address unlisted). By December Mr. & Mrs. Lee Wilkey were hired as the new Ranch Managers and the foundation herd of Herefords from Albert K. Mitchell had arrived at the Ranch.[21]

The first full year of operations at the Boys Ranch was 1947—and as a watershed year it provides us with a review of the progress. Al Buck seems to sum up the Directors' position nicely when he writes:

All of us are busy people, and what time has been devoted to this program has of necessity, been torn out of days already too crowded to permit thorough study of countless problems in connection with this and other matters; and yet in spite of pressures we have believed it imperative to further this project and help it to achieve the success it merits.[22]

Virtually every member of the Board of Directors was a busy successful businessman yet each devoted hours of time to the needs of the Ranch. While the majority of the Board favored placing the permanent Ranch buildings on the west side of State Highway #47, the land problem was a real consideration. It was now becoming evident that the cost of land improvement was far greater than the money which they had or would have for some time. In fact, even the leveling equipment arrived late and thus the spring planting, so vital to a ranch, was late. The foundation herd of herefords given by Albert Mitchell were augmented by five more white-face calves given by George Currier of Artesia.

Construction included completing the hog shed and a rat-proof storage building. Mr. Wilkey converted the horse shed into a brooder house for the baby chicks donated by a Mr. Clark. The feed and necessary equipment for the chickens was given to the Ranch by the North Albuquerque Lions Club and a poultry operation was underway by April. Time was being given to fencing whenever possible. The division fence along the north boundary was completed, after which a fence running north to south and dividing the first large pasture was started. "Starting from scratch is a very expensive procedure, especially when so many items are in short supply and prices are very high. Alfalfa seed alone cost nearly $600."[23]

During 1947 down at White Sands the military was busy testing missiles reaching 78 miles altitude and 3,000 miles per hour. Meanwhile, with five boys at the Ranch, the Directors continued to pursue their established policy of taking the boys slowly and waiting for the last one to become fairly well assimilated before admitting another boy. The "founding fathers" philosophy is embedded in the following words:

> We have always held that all our efforts were in vain, if the boys did not have the feeling of security that came from being loved and wanted in as nearly a normal home atmosphere as could be provided for them; and we were convinced of the wisdom of admitting new boys slowly. But it has been hard to resist the impulse to take them too fast, knowing their need and their eagerness to come here.[24]

New boys were slowly but steadily being added to the Ranch family. Records list the following boys: Claude (no address given), Benny and Robert (ages 13 and 10 from Santa Fe), Clarence (12 years old from Hobbs), Edwin (no age or address), Buddie (age 10 of Roswell), Billy (age 13 of Gallup), Frank (age 10 from Albuquerque), Anthony (age 9 from Albuquerque), and John (no age given of Jemez Springs).

While the boys were coming from all over the state and from all kinds of backgrounds such as broken homes, alcoholic parents, elderly grandparents, etc., not all could be reached. For example, the Committee on Admission reported in July that a young man who had been recommended to the Ranch had just been committed to the State Industrial School. It appears that he ran away from the Detention Home in Albuquerque and was arrested in Las Cruces where the judge of the Juvenile Court committed him.

As the number of boys at the Ranch increased it was obvious that the Wilkeys had their hands full and would need to have some help. In April, a Mr. and Mrs. Ernest Thompson were hired as farmer and cook on a trial basis for $100 per month plus room and board. Apparently, this did not work out to everyone's satisfaction for the Thompsons were discharged in August. At that time a Mrs. Thomason was hired as the cook with the same salary.

As the number of boys increased it was also recognized that schooling would have to be started at the Ranch. To that end an old CCC (Civilian Conservation Corps) building located at Camp Luna, near Las Vegas, was purchased, taken down, and moved to the Ranch. Lack of a school teacher and the funds to pay for one prevented setting up a school at the Ranch. By the fall of 1947 there were thirteen boys at the Ranch with most of them attending school at La Joya.

Detailed reading of all the available committee reports leads one to conclude that nothing came easy in those early years. Indeed at times it must have seemed as if heaven itself was unsure about this operation. Consider that during 1947 there was a water shortage which seriously affected all of the crops. The vegetable garden proved almost a complete failure, nearly all the young fruit trees died, the cotton crop was nipped by frost, and the rye crop never came up. Even the animals were not immune from this streak of bad luck, for one of the registered heifers donated by Al Mitchell died as a result of having eaten a small piece of wire which pierced her heart.

Difficult days? You bet! Yet in spite of all the adversities there was not only perseverance but even a sense of humor. For example, there was the continuous problem of discouraging the boys from drinking out of the ditches. However, in July when all the boys completed their typhoid inoculations without even one getting a reaction Al Buck humorously remarked that, "This made us wonder whether slurping water from the ditches on the sly had enabled them to acquire immunity."[25] Progress could even be measured in interesting ways. The annual report states that, "The oldest boy, whose shoe size was seven when he came to the Ranch, found he needed 11D, when he came into town for another pair. His feet had grown four full sizes in eight months."[26]

It is interesting to note that the Cattle Sanitary Board advised the Ranch to change its cattle brand, substituting for the Flying BR, which would remain a holding brand, the BAR LAZY A. Backward Seven. Records indicate that the boys never showed the slightest interest in this brand. So that by making the Flying BR with two irons, the first brand was reinstated, and the Ranch still used the Flying BR brand.

Public relations were greatly improved when the staff from Radio Station KOAT came to the Ranch to do a series of six fifteen-minute broadcasts. The first recording was made at the Ranch on July 18, 1948 using magnetic tape. It was called "A Day at the Flying BR," and was broadcast the following night.

In addition more and more people were becoming interested in the program. More service clubs like the Elks and Lions came to the Ranch for an afternoon visit and stayed for supper. Photos of Ranch activities were being shown at several state conventions. That the state was becoming aware of the Ranch was certain and that all kinds of people wanted to help was a fact. Sometimes the results were indeed strange. For example, on one occasion the operator of a restaurant in Old Town, known as Rita's-on-the-Plaza sent letters to Albuquerque citizens (without first obtaining permission from the Ranch) telling them that the entire proceeds from certain days would be given to the Boys Ranch. However, when an accounting was asked for, the owner was unable to fulfill their commitment. The Board acted wisely on this matter. "There was not time for a discussion of this matter, which came up at 1:55 p.m., the time decided upon for adjournment. The meeting was adjourned at 1:56 p.m."[27]

Throughout the year money was a serious problem and as he did on numerous occasions, when the finances were the bleakest, Al Buck would loan the operation money from his own funds. In December, the belated campaign for funds was made with a series of four letters being sent out to those who had previously contributed. The year ended with fourteen boys being housed at the Ranch with one set of houseparents and a cook. There was so much work to be done in getting established that not even time could be spared for the close supervision required. "We need more money, more personnel, and the genuine interest of more people throughout the State."[28]

In retrospect today we can see that much was accomplished that first full year and much progress was made. The group of boys being cared for was small because everything was new and funds were scarce. This was truly a pioneering period and those who dedicated their time, services and interest were truly pioneers. In the words of Al Buck, "A fine start has been made. Let us rededicate ourselves as we enter upon the second year's activities, pledging an even greater measure of devotion to this preventive program of boys' training, for the future welfare of our state and our nation."[29]

At the January 12, 1948 meeting of the Creditors and Advisors held at the El Fidel Hotel in Albuquerque, the Secretary reported that $8,500 had been contributed so far in the appeal for funds. In addition $637 was contributed by six Elks lodges and that the Belen Merchants basketball team was playing a benefit game, the proceeds of which would go to the Boys Ranch.

New boys, such as Jean Long, who was also known as Jean Thompson and as Jean Milbourne (which makes one wonder if the boy even knew who he was) age 12 of Carlsbad, and Tony, age 11 of Albuquerque were admitted to the Ranch. Two of the early boys, Lee of Carlsbad and Jackie formerly of Belen, were officially discharged after almost two years when they were viewed as "hopeless." Obviously not every boy could be helped.

During the first week of January, the Executive Secretary Charles Minton and his wife took complete charge of the Ranch in order to give the Wilkeys their first ever vacation. While the minutes reflect the official

"Thank You" to the Ranch family for their faithful devotion to their duties it was already evident to insiders that problems of all kinds were arising at the Ranch faster than they could be solved.

To say that there was a shortage of help, a constant turnover of personnel and usually a shortage of funds is to put it too simply. In a seven-page memorandum to the Board, Charles Minton detailed the entire situation. Stock was being neglected, buildings were unclean, fields were neglected, punishment was excessive, leadership was not being promoted, boys were running away and on and on went the problems. A reading of the situation reveals a Ranch mother that was very nervous and seriously ill. At the same time the Ranch father was a strict disciplinarian of the old school. These boys were not angels, in fact far from it. Many boys were nervous and high strung. Most were not brought up to be courteous and the majority were difficult to manage. What was not evident at the Ranch at this time was a good example of leadership. Perhaps had the Wilkeys been younger or better trained, things would have worked out better. What happened was that after a blistering exchange of letters which resolved little, the Wilkeys resigned in May. They took several months off, reconsidered the job and reapplied for the position in September at which time they were turned down.

Meanwhile, a change in board membership was occurring. Unfortunately several of the early board members became disturbed by the negativism that seemed to be occurring and resigned. Perhaps the most regretted resignation was that of Albert Mitchell who was the Chairman of the Ranch Management Committee. All in all probably the constant pressure and changing scene was just too time consuming for a number of businessmen. In any case new names began to appear in the records of the Board of Directors.

The first professional fund raising effort got underway with the hiring of the Wells Organization of Texas. It attempted to raise $250,000 before the end of 1948. A Mr. Kenneth J. Brooks actually directed the local campaign which ran for sixty days from December 15, 1948 until February 15, 1949. To expedite this money-raising effort the Executive Board of the Corporation in April was authorized to "organize a corporation not for profit to be known as the New Mexico Boys Ranch Foundation, which would receive monies and other assets for investment and for the payment of operating expenses of the New Mexico Boys Ranch."[30]

At this same meeting the President stated that the bills for the past three months were delinquent and that some $12,000 was owed. The new Corporation was authorized to borrow up to $24,000 on a promissory note from the Albuquerque National Trust and Savings Bank to be signed by ten endorsers. These men were literally putting their businesses and reputations on the line for the future of the Ranch.

Fall of 1948 found Mr. & Mrs. James Lee Southall of Las Cruces being hired for the positions of Ranch father and mother. Mr. Southall was soon to be a graduate of New Mexico A&M and Mrs. Southall had completed two years of college at Eastern New Mexico. Both had farm and ranch backgrounds, came highly recommended and were considerably younger (he was 27 and she was 24) than the previous family. Their salary was set at $300 a month plus living expenses.

Records indicate an increase in the number of boys at the Ranch during the fall and each came with a special story.

RAMON—age 9 from Santa Fe. Listed as a wayward boy who ran away from home and wanders in the mountains. The mother was dead and the father brought home women from time to time as "step-mothers." They were unsympathetic to the boy, who would then run off.

JOHN—age 11 from Albuquerque. No mother and the father, a veteran of World War I, asked the American Legion Post in Albuquerque for help.

CLYDE—age 10 from Deming. Mental test of IQ was 80. Father killed in the Pacific and mother living with another man. Roams the streets and has been expelled from school.

FRANK—age 12 of Albuquerque, had been in the court several times and was at the time of admission. He had congenital syphilis and was admitted with the understanding that he receive blood tests and treatment every three months to be sure that he would not be infectious.[31]

A series of news releases from the Ranch that hit the wire services before the end of the year showed that an optimistic era was beginning to emerge.

- The Posse Club of Truth or Consequences collected $500 for the Ranch and plans to return to help dedicate the new Quonset hut dining room and kitchen.
- The Albuquerque Optimist Club entertained 12 Boys Ranch boys at their regular luncheon at the Hilton Hotel.
- Girl Scout Troop #23 of Albuquerque spent a day at Boys Ranch.
- The New Mexico Boys Ranch is getting a new look. In one day recently, 100 fruit trees and shrubbery were planted around the main dormitories.[32]

Two significant events occurred during the year 1949, one of which was expected and one was not. After several years of discussion and one actual interview a contract was signed with Thomas and Phyllis Summers to begin work on June 10th as school teachers at the Ranch. Each teacher was hired for the year at $2,100 payable in monthly installments of $175 together with living expenses.

While the terminology of the contracts are virtually exact there were some differences. For example, while both were to teach elementary and secondary school subjects, Mr. Summers was "in addition, to instruct the boys in shop work and the proper use of shop equipment as well as such other manual arts provided for in the training program at the Ranch as he is qualified to teach; also to furnish leadership in farm and ranch activities, 4-H Club work and in supervised play and recreation." The contract goes on to say that, "said teacher further agrees to help see the boys through their chores and in cases of disability of the Ranch father, to assume whatever additional duties are necessary for the duration of the emergency."[33]

Apparently, Mrs. Summers' day began at 8:00 a.m,. while Mr. Summers' contract specifically states that, "the day's duties will commence at the boy's rising time in the morning and will end with the conclusion of the evening meal."[34] Thus at last real educators were installed at the Ranch itself to help with these young boys. It is interesting to note that each contract stated that the teacher "will not in any way attempt to indoctrinate in them any sectarian religious beliefs and will not influence them in the adoption of any denomination or sectarian religion different from their own."[35] This religious freedom has been strictly adhered to down through the years.

Given the nature of the boys being admitted that year the Ranch needed all the educational help it could get. The following are examples of boys being admitted.

> ALBERT—From Clovis, no age given. State that he is wayward and the home situation is bad.

> GERALD—10 years old from Santa Fe. Wayward and difficult to control. Father deserted the family. Boy living with Aunt and Uncle.

> WAYNE—11 years old of Hobbs. Father's where-abouts unknown. Mother and stepfather separated.

> DONALD—12 years old of Las Cruces. Mother ill and cannot care for him. Stepfather away much of the time.

> GEORGE & CHARLES—(brothers) ages 7 and 9. Poor home situation and boys are becoming unmanageable.

> JOHN—age 12 of Albuquerque. Very bad home conditions. Mother working all day. Father is loafing. Much tensions and strain in the house.

And the kind of story that broke the heart of those who did the admitting.

> JACK—age 12 of Albuquerque. Caught stealing from home (although not outside). Brutally beaten by step-father to the point that the boy was placed in the Detention Home to protect him. Stepfather was sentenced to ten days in jail and fined. He was charged with assault and battery on this boy.

The list of troubled and unwanted boys goes on and on.

> CASEY—age 13 of Albuquerque. Oldest of five children all

of whom have been abandoned by both parents whose
whereabouts are unknown.

GEORGE & WALTER—11 and 13 respectfully of Portales.
Mother unable to adequately feed and cope with them.
They are undernourished and getting out of control.[36]

It was soon obvious that there was almost a wave of neglected and
abused young boys in the State of New Mexico that needed the help of
the Boys Ranch. That this job was rapidly expanding and demanded
more and more is signalled by the resignation of Charles Minton, the
Executive Secretary in June. Minton had given untold hours to the
starting of the Ranch and his work was to be missed. However, time
marches on and the list of boys needing help did not seem to shorten.

In a reorganization move Harold MacGibbon was named Business
Manager and James Southall was appointed Ranch Manager in charge of
all operations at the Ranch. In order not to repeat the earlier mistake of
mixed lines of authority, Southall reported directly to Al Buck.

Expansion was the order of the day with plans being made to enlarge
the bunk house. To this end a statewide campaign was conducted during
the summer months. More and more New Mexico towns and cities were
being asked to contribute to the Boys Ranch. It must have been pleasant
news on that August day to hear President Buck say: "I think the Board
of Directors may congratulate themselves that the stability and per-
manence of the New Mexico Boys Ranch is absolutely assured."[37]

That the Ranch was being recognized on its own merit is evident by
the fact that Governor Mabry requested a representative of the Boys
Ranch be appointed to a State Committee on Child and Youth. Mr.
Homer Lawrence was appointed to this assignment.[38]

Considerable pressure was building for more rapid expansion and
Mr. O.S. Greaser, a board member expressed what others apparently
were thinking when he said, "that some dissatisfaction had been voiced
among people who had contacted him, making criticism of the fact that
we had been in operation for approximately five years and only had
facilities for eighteen or twenty boys."[39] The feeling seemed to be that an
immediate expansion of dormitory space should be made and more
boys should be admitted immediately. It was hoped that by taking in
more boys both the present donors as well as the non-donors would be

stimulated into action. The fall (1949) Expansion Fund Drive was for this purpose.

Perhaps it was due to the pressure felt by the Ranch to increase its size or perhaps it was just circumstance, none the less, Fall saw the admission of some truly troubled boys.

For example, a boy named Cheston was in serious trouble before the Juvenile Court. The admissions committee was told that unless he was admitted to the Ranch he would be sent to Springer (Industrial School). Considerable discussion was held because the boy was already sixteen years old. Cecil Pragnell moved that Article 17 (age limit) be amended for this particular case and it was. Cheston was brought before the Board and told of his options. While on one hand he was too old to associate with the boys already at the Ranch it was hoped that he could become a leader and do some good.[40] As the saying goes, "the best laid plans of mice and men often go astray" and so it was in this case. By October this young man had violated the conditions of his acceptance on several occasions. The final straw came when this young man left the Ranch premises and, with other boys, stole honey from hives of a nearby ranch. He was removed from the Ranch and no further mention of him is made. It became obvious that the Boys Ranch could not help every boy. That many other were helped in these difficult days is almost a miracle in itself. The boys kept coming.

> GEORGE—from Socorro, (no age given), held in jail for several weeks due to his participation in the theft of a horse. The owner refused to press charges providing the Ranch would take him. Mr. Pragnell picked him up at the Courthouse in Socorro and delivered him to the Ranch.

> ROBERTO—Old Albuquerque, had been turned over to his grandfather at birth; a constant truant from school and had been sent to the Detention Home several times.

> MICHAEL—Albuquerque, turned over to his grandfather after the death of his father. Truant from school and charged with bicycle theft.

> JESSE—Tucumcari, parents divorced, sister in a Welfare Home. Mother and son live in small, undesirable one room.

Not enough income to take care of them both.

And on and on.

Story One: EZEKIEL ULIBARRI

Ezekiel Ulibarri lives in Veguita, a small predominantly Hispanic village near the present day site of the Boys Ranch. He was one of the first laborers hired by the Ranch to help construct the very first building. People connected with the Ranch refer to Mr. Ulibarri as "the man who remembers the early years." Ulibarri worked at the Ranch for over twenty years and became known affectionately as "Señor Shorty." What follows are excerpts from an oral history interview taken when he was 85 years young.

Ezekiel, meaning the prophet, Ulibarri was born on April 10, 1907 five years before New Mexico became a state. He was the youngest of a very large family and his father died when he was eight years old. Apparently his father died at about the same time that a distant aunt also died. After a few years, the uncle and his mother, a Martinez, received permission from the archbishop to marry, thus merging the two families. As "Señor Shorty" says, "they married and they make a happy life. They were about eight (children) of one part and about eight (children) of another part. They was a big people!"

Ulibarri's ancestors may well go back to the earliest Spanish settlers in New Mexico. Perhaps even to Spain as one of his relatives is currently trying to research. It is utterly fascinating to hear "Señor Shorty" recall stories of his father and uncle hauling freight up from El Paso, Texas (and maybe even from Chihuahua) by wagons and yoked oxen. It is hypothetically possible that Shorty's father was born (Shorty does not know the date) while the Rio Grande Valley was still a part of Mexico. In any case "Señor Shorty" vividly recalls how his father's big plows and oxen helped make the irrigation ditches of the area.

Years later he served as a mayordomo (water governor) and was very involved with the "politicos." As "Señor Shorty" says, "I been the Republican all my life." The living room walls of his house are lined with certificates from the soil conservation agency in Santa Fe and other various political agencies.

When he started farming he lived alone for awhile and as he states, "that time it was pretty hard to live on or to do anything." At the age of twenty-five he married Soylita Baca who was then seventeen. Over the years they had twelve children, though losing six babies and a set of twins. The house in which he was interviewed in was built in 1924 by he and his brother using "terrones bricks." This is the reason why "Señor Shorty" was hired by the Boys Ranch—he could make the "terrones."

Author: When did you first become acquainted with the Boys Ranch?

Ulibarri: What I remember is that there was an old house over there (meaning on the ranch land) and nobody lives on it. This Mr. Andrew Gordon (the 1st Ranch Manager) . . . he was the "Pop," they call him "Pop." Now they are the managers, you know? He come over here and ask me if I want to work with the Boys Ranch. I say, "all right." This I think was in April '46.

Author: Then at that time there was no real ranch there, right?

Ulibarri: (drinks some more coffee and reflects) Finally, he says, "we used to get water over there to fill our barrels for the men that were taking care of the sheep." (Apparently they would stop at the land on the way out to wherever the sheep were kept at that time.) Shorty adds, "nothing was there when we began to make the well and the adobes." He remembers something and says, "there was a funny thing, there was two little holes (old wells) on a high place. One had nice good water and one was salty!"

Author: I have been told that you were the first to start making the "terrones bricks" used in the first building. Would you please explain what had to be done to make such a brick?

Ulibarri: We just cut the sod with chisels or shovel and then turn them over (to dry). The ground has the grass and roots in it. It was so wet around that it was almost like glue. They (the Ranch) paid people either four cents or two cents to run the wagons (per trip?). My son says, "Daddy, why don't you let me go over there?" So he went and he'd put about twenty or thirty "terrones" on that little wagon and take them over there and come back. He hauled more than the man's in the wagon!

Author: **Who did the actual building of the first building?**

Ulibarri: I almost do it all, not all, there were others working on it. I had been taking care of the farm work when Mr. Gordon says, "Oh, Shorty, why'd you let me farm and you go over there and (build)." When asked about farming Shorty replied, "well, on the Boy's Ranch we used to raise when I started working, alfalfa, corn and one time we planted a little beans and vegetables, tomatoes and things like that."

Author: **Ever raise chilies? (this being a very important crop in New Mexico)**

Ulibarri: On the Boys Ranch we don't ever raise any but I have a nephew—he plant about forty acres.

Author: **Did you ever raise cotton?**

Ulibarri: (His answer is a fascinating piece of history.) "Yeah, I used to raised cotton and we use to have help from Mexico. They called them 'braceros'" (this was the name for the temporary Mexican laborers during World War II). Shorty went on to say, "we got to make like a contract to bring them over here. They (the government) send them to Socorro and I would go there and pick them up."

While official records say very little about Mr. Andrew Gordon, the first Ranch Manager, it is interesting to note that Shorty remembers him as a man that bought a big piece of land between La Joya and the site of the Boys Ranch. Records do indicate that at the time of construction of the Boys Ranch the road, now known as New Mexico Route #47, was dirt and not paved. "Señor Shorty" said, "We had to get a driver to go pick up a load of sand for use on the road" (to fill in the holes). It should also be noted that there were no telephones in the area at this time.

The present day visitor to the Boys Ranch who drives down I-25 and crosses the Rio Grande River at the Bernardo bridge might find it interesting to reflect on the way it used to be. For example, Shorty Ulibarri remembers that when he was young the wagon road came down from Belen to La Joya where they forded the river to go on to Socorro. This was in warm weather and in the winter they would cross over on the ice. Shorty's wonderful memory came through when asked about the bridge at Bernardo.

Author: Has there always been a bridge across the Rio at Bernardo?

Ulibarri: The first (bridge) was a wooden bridge, then an iron bridge and now the big concrete bridge. In 1941 I worked eight months to rebuild it. It was hard to get work at that time. A Republican cannot get no jobs like that. When the Republicans get in, I guess they pass on with the same (this is really a comment on partisan politics New Mexican style a la the 1930s-1940s). One man (a local politico) tell the boss something and the next Monday they give me pretty hard work for the start—making a big hole. (Apparently he means digging out the rocks for the bridge abutments). In a few days they make me a carpenter and I make a lot of those corners on the bridge all the way in to Bernardo (he means the wooden forms into which the concrete was poured). Shorty laughed when he remembered the day that the gang boss didn't like one of his corners. He proceeded to take it apart and broke the frame in the process. When the "Big Boss" showed up he did not like the new form and had Shorty put his old one back in place.[41]

NOTES:

1. *Minutes First Meeting of Incorporators* New Mexico Boys Ranch. Official Document New Mexico Boys Ranch. (Hereafter referred to as N.M.B.R.)
2. *Certificate of Incorporation.*
3. Minutes, Boys Ranch Board of Directors, October 3, 1944.
4. Ibid.
5. Ibid.
6. Minutes, Boys Ranch Board of Directors, October 31, 1944.
7. Ibid.
8. Minutes, Boys Ranch Board of Directors, December 19 , 1944.
9. Minutes, Boys Ranch Board of Directors, March 12, and March 19, 1944.
10. Report on Visit to Chadwick Site, April 9, 1945. Unpublished Documents, N.M.B.R.
11. Ibid.
12. Minutes of Directors and Advisors Meeting, May 7, 1945.
13. Minutes of Directors and Advisors Meeting, November 16, 1945.
14. Treasurer's Report, January 28, 1946. N.M.B.R. Documents.
15. Minutes of the Board of Directors and Advisors Meeting, February 19, 1946.
16. Minutes of the Board of Directors and Advisors Meeting, February 19, 1946.
17. Meeting of the Executive Board, September 12, 1946.
18. Letter from Al Buck to Andrew Gordon dated September 13, 1946.
19. Minutes of the Executive Board Meeting, October 8, 1946.
20. Albuquerque Journal, February 2, 1990.
21. Minutes from the Committee on Admissions, November 4 and December 2, 1946.
22. Second Annual Meeting, The Flying BR, February 9, 1948.
23. Ibid.
24. Ibid., p. 2.
25. Ibid, p. 2.
26. Ibid.
27. Executive Board Minutes, April 3, 1947.
28. Second Annual Report, op. cit., p. 6.
29. Op. cit., p. 6.
30. Minutes of the Meeting of Directors and Advisors, April 26, 1948.

31. Meeting of Committee on Admissions Spring-Summer 1948.
32. New Releases 1948 N.M.B.R. Files.
33. Teacher Contracts, Boys Ranch Files.
34. Ibid.
35. Ibid.
36. All of these boys names and stories appear in various forms in the files of the Boys Ranch.
37. Minutes of the Board of Directors & Advisors, August 15, 1949.
38. Ibid.
39. Op. cit.
40. Meeting of the Board of Advisors, August 24, 1949.
41. Interview with Ezekiel Ulibarri, May 25, 1992, Veguita, New Mexico.

Chapter Three
THE AL BUCK TRAGEDY

There was no Annual Meeting of the Board held in 1949 due to the fact that the Ranch was in the midst of the Expansion Fund Campaign and everyone was very busy. However, by January 30, 1950 the Board reported that they had secured pledges and payments totalling $278,754.87.[1] In round numbers the total cost of this campaign was $54,000 of which $19,740 was paid to the Wells Organization. The balance of $34,260 represents office rent, clerical personnel, artist, maps, brochures, newspaper mats, stationery, postage, traveling expenses, et cetera.[2] The success of this tremendous effort is felt in these words by President Al Buck.

> There have been dark days, but we have weathered the storm and due to the generous response of our patrons throughout the State, we have been able to pay off all but $8,000 of the bank loan ($24,000) and reduce a personal loan by one of the Directors (himself), made in September '48 to start the campaign, from $10,000 to $5,000.[3]

Next to money, or rather the lack of it, the other major problem in these early years concerned the rapid turnover of Ranch personnel. For example, in June of 1949 Charles Minton resigned as Executive-Secretary due to poor health. He was replaced by Harold R. MacGibbon who was given the title of Business Manager and Secretary. Two months later Mr. & Mrs. James L. Southall resigned as Ranch Parents in order to return to college. The Southalls had only been at the Ranch for one year.

In addition the school at the Ranch turned out to be an ongoing problem. In June, 1949 Mr. & Mrs. Thomas Summers were hired as teachers and almost immediately Mr. Summers had numerous problems. By September Summers was seriously ill and was admitted to the Veterans Hospital, after which he resigned. Next came Robert Lefgren who apparently was only qualified to teach Physical Education. In turn he was succeeded by Mr. Lauri Koski who turned out to be a poor disciplinarian and his services were terminated in January, 1950. At this point it appears that the experiment of a "Ranch School" pretty much ended. Arrangements were made with the County of Socorro to send the boys to school at La Joya. At first the public school bus picked up and returned the boys to the Ranch. Sometime later the Ranch acquired its own bus and the school district reimbursed them for mileage. Present day readers will find it amazing to learn that each boy was served a hot lunch at La Joya for the sum of 20 cents per boy per month.

With the departure of the Southalls Mrs. Clarah Yoder became the cook, practical nurse and general housekeeper. Wayne Bartholomew became the Ranch Superintendent working under the leadership of MacGibbon. Bartholomew organized an active 4-H Club which worked hard for the livestock and poultry exhibits at the State Fair. Prizes were received for a Guernsey bull calf (Junior Championship), wool (Junior Championship and a first price at the Denver Stock Show), as well as first prizes on range fat lamb, hogs, poultry and rabbits. Obviously somebody, or should we say, a lot of somebodies were doing some fine work.

Through the generosity of O.E. Beck the Ranch acquired a four ton York freezer and with some donated lumber from the Ingram Lumber Company built their own cooling room. This eliminated the costs of rented lockers in Belen. The dairy barn was completed including facilities for washing and sterilizing milk equipment. A milk cooling system was installed and the garage was converted into a laundry. This last action may seem mundane, however it saved the Ranch between $35 and $50 per month on laundry bills plus the transportation costs to Albuquerque. Perhaps the most appreciated purchase was that of a 16mm sound movie projector which was used both for education and entertainment.

Optimism was running high by early 1950 for it appeared that all phases of the Ranch were improving. When a Ranch donor asked what was the maximum number of boys the Ranch hoped to accommodate in the future President Buck replied, "When the program was completed it was to be from two to three hundred."[4] Already there was the request from the Probation officer of Dona Ana County requesting the raising of the age limit to 17 years of age for admission. After considerable discussion this idea was rejected and the age limits continued to be restricted from 7 years to 14 years. It was hoped that with a new dormitory the Ranch would be able to accommodate fifty-four boys. The boys kept coming:

CLIFFORD—Albuquerque, no age given, difficult home life.

ARTHUR—Hot Springs, difficult home life.

THOMAS—Albuquerque, excessive drinking by step-father, mother separating again. Mother agreed to $30 per month support.

TROY—Clovis, father a farm laborer who lives in a truck. Boy spends most of his time on the streets in bad company.

In some cases the boy being considered for admission got in trouble too quickly and too deeply to even make it to the Ranch. For example, a young man named Rudolph who was committed to the Industrial School at Springer and was investigated by Manager MacGibbon who then recommended admission on a trial basis. However, when released he broke his parole agreement and was re-committed to Springer before arriving at the Ranch. Any discussion of the admissions process should include the fact that each boy was examined both physically and mentally before any decision was made on their acceptance. The health records of these early boys was exceptionally good and their medical and dental care was generously furnished by the following professionals: Drs. Adler, Rader and Beck of Albuquerque; Drs. Rivas and Wier of Belen and Dr. Manser a dentist in Albuquerque.

On March 5, 1950 the following were elected officers of the organization:

President	- A.E. Buck
Vice-President	- Carl Brogan
Treasurer	- Glenn L. Emmons
Secretary.	- H.R. MacGibbon

The number of officers of the corporation was increased at this time by adding two Vice-Presidents. They were:

Roy K. Stovall and James Robertson.[5]

During these early years the Ranch Board was divided into six working committees. These were: (1) Building, (2) Ranch Management, (3) Education and Recreation, (4) Admission and Personnel, (5) Furnishings and Equipment, and (6) Finance. It should be mentioned that at this time the majority of the board members were from Albuquerque. For example, all nine members of the Admission and Personnel Committee were from that city. Other areas of the State were represented by members from Socorro, Belen, State College (Las Cruces), Carlsbad, Clovis, Hot Springs, Las Vegas, and Gallup. People holding special positions were sought out and placed on certain committees. For example, J.C. Jaramillo Superintendent of the La Joya Public Schools, Dan Miranda Principal of Belen High School and L.S. Kurtz State 4-H Club Leader from State College were placed on the Education and Recreation Committee. The point is that from the very beginning the Board has always attempted to have a broad base of committee support in all phases of the Ranch operation.

While construction of the new dormitory was underway the New Mexico Federation of Women's Clubs pledged $5,000 towards the construction of a chapel. In April, with summer vacation just around the corner, Richard Barela, a teacher at La Joya Public Schools, was hired as the Ranch's first recreation leader. He worked evenings during the school year and his salary was paid by the school district. Buried deep in committee notes is this following wonderful statement:

Mr. Barela, Mr. Harp (Ranch Manager), and Mrs. Dudrey (Ranch Mother) stated that the recreation period as planned after supper had not been too satisfactory as it had made the boys late for bed, and had excited them so that it was difficult for them to go to sleep.[6]

It was stated that there were about twenty-five boys at the Ranch. Half being from eight to eleven years old and half from eleven to fourteen. Obviously all of them were full of energy.

On June 15, 1950 Malcolm Long and his wife were hired to be the

Ranch Family and in complete charge of everything except construction. Throughout the summer the boys kept on coming:

CELSO—Gallup, age unknown, oldest of six children, father deserted the family and mother was on relief. The boy worked part time until he got in trouble.

RICHARD—Albuquerque, father an alcoholic who deserted the family. Boy was sent to a military school for awhile, then stole a bicycle and was in a detention home.

DONALD—Tucumcari, age thirteen, father died of illness contacted during WWII. Mother could not care for him and was currently living on a remotely located ranch. That ranch owner had agreed to pay $30.00 a month for his board.

JOHNNY—Age 10, born out of wedlock, lacked a proper home, arrested for the theft of food.

Sometimes the parents of these boys did get their personal lives in order. "Tommy A. was released to his mother as requested for she can now provide him with a congenial and normal surroundings."[7]

The minutes of the August 14, 1950 meeting refer to E.M. Ulibarri as, "A farm laborer and faithful and competent employee for much of the time since the beginning of the project." Mr. Ulibarri known affectionately as "Señor Shorty" by those at the Ranch was one of the most interesting people interviewed by this author. His special story of these early years is told as Story One in the Second Chapter.

World events such as the Korean War are reflected in the Boys Ranch records from time to time. For example, on August 23, 1950 board member James M. Robertson was forced to resign due to his recall by the Armed Forces. Racial integration was already included at the Ranch in October as the applications for admission included "a colored boy from Albuquerque."[8]

Ranch managers changed once again in late 1950 with the departure of the Long family. MacGibbon also resigned but agreed to stay on until January 15, 1951. At that time all management was consolidated under the leadership of Cecil Pragnell who was the former Bernalillo County Agricultural Agent (see Story Two). In his resignation letter MacGibbon laid his finger on one of the problems that had troubled the

Ranch since its inception. He wrote, "If the project is to accomplish the purposes for which it was established, it is necessary to have personnel that is trained and capable of analyzing each boy's mind and applying the necessary technique to correct the undesirable complexities that their past experiences have instilled in their young minds."[9]

On Sunday April 1, 1951 some one hundred and fifty people from the Board of Directors, the Albuquerque Heights Lions Club and various invited guests gathered at the Ranch for a celebration of accomplishment. The festive gathering was told that the old school building had been moved and would be stuccoed to conform with the dormitory. Then it would be made into a kitchen, dining room, and living quarters. The building on the hill was to become the living quarters for Mr. Pragnell and the laundry was to be moved into the empty quonset hut.

This large group was further informed that "the New Mexico Boys Ranch had given the State of New Mexico 32 acres of land for the highway now being put through the Ranch (Route #47). Fences and cattle guards should be provided by the State but they haven't been."[10] At the same time a Mrs. Patten from Gallup announced that the Federation of Women's Clubs would not be carrying on with the Chapel Fund and that the money ($5,000) could be used for other projects. Al Buck apparently hoped to keep the fund intact for a future chapel.[11] J.C. Jaramillo, State Senator and Superintendent of the La Joya Schools spoke on how happy he was to have the boys at his school, that no state money was received for their education and that their lunches were now free.[12]

From time to time throughout history tragic events do occur that totally alter an entire situation. So it was with the very unfortunate death of Al Buck on June 23, 1951. According to all reports Buck and his wife Lydia were returning to New Mexico from the Republican National Convention in St. Louis, Missouri. As the result of a violent thunderstorm their small airplane crashed and burned near Clinton, Oklahoma. At the time of his heartbreaking death Al Buck was forty-nine years old and was considered by all as the prime moving force behind the Boys Ranch.

So keenly felt was this tragedy that not a single note appears in the Ranch record books for the next six months. It is indeed fortunate for the Boys Ranch that Roy K. Stovall, of Truth or Consequences, was able to step in and provide the necessary leadership. At the time of this transition Stovall was considered one of New Mexico's famous cattlemen and was the former Vice-President of the Cattle-Growers Association. During his leadership he organized a Boys Ranch Sheriff's Posse which was patterned after his own Sierra County Sheriff's Posse. He devoted a lot of personal time training the boys who wanted to ride with the Posse (one of those boys was John Holmbach, see Story Three). Ill health forced Stovall to curtail his activities with Boys Ranch in June of 1953.

In a fascinating two-page report to Stovall from the Committee on Admissions we have the first real profile of these young boys. Some of the statistics from that February 11, 1952 report are as follows:

DURATION OF STAY - Of the 77 boys at the Ranch, 55 were admitted in the year 1951, 35 of that number having been admitted after July 1st. Records on date of admission are incomplete as to 7 of the boys. Only one has been at the Ranch since 1947. Six of these now there were admitted in 1949, and three of those now there were admitted in 1950. Two have been admitted in 1952, one of whom, Sherwood Graham, had previously been at the Ranch from March to September, 1951. This boy was taken away by his mother, and ran away from her in January of this year, and was returned by his maternal aunts for re-admission to the Ranch.

AGE GROUPS - We have at the Ranch one boy aged 7, one aged 8, four aged 9, three aged 10, 8 aged 11, eleven aged 12, eighteen aged 13, fifteen aged 14, nine aged 15, and three aged 16. It is apparent from this that group activities will have to be worked out appropriately to age groups.

ETHNIC DISTRIBUTION - Distribution has been made in three categories which are the principal race groups in New Mexico, namely, Anglo, Spanish American, and Negro. We have at the Ranch 26 Anglo boys, 47 Spanish American, and 2 Negroes. Records are incomplete on two. (The omission of Native Americans from the list of racial groups may be a sign of those times or it may just be an error in the records.)

PREVIOUS CUSTODY - Classification has been made under

four categories, namely; (1) Father; (2) Mother; (3) Both parents; (4) Neither parent, but a relative. The father had previous custody of 24 of the boys; the mother had previous custody of 32; both parents had previous custody of 6; a relative other than father or mother had previous custody of 8, and aunt accounting for 3 of these, a grandfather for 3, a foster father for 1, and a sister for 1. Records are incomplete on the others.

POLICE RECORDS - Twelve of the boys had police records previous to admission to the Ranch, 61 had none, 1 was sent to the Ranch as an alternative to being confined at Springer, and records were incomplete on the others. Of those with police records, 2 had been arrested once, 1 twice, 1 three times, 2 four times, 1 five times and 3 six times. One was described as a chronic wrongdoer, but his police record is not set out, nor is the police record of the one sent to the Ranch in lieu of Springer.[13]

By September it was noted that delinquent pledges amounting to $52,000 were due the Ranch. In an attempt to solve that problem an office was set up at 115 Third Street, N.W. in Albuquerque. Mrs. Helen Speaker was hired to serve both as a secretary and in charge of the publicity campaign. To that end one of her accomplishments was to start the first Boys Ranch newsletter. It was called The Tattling Tumbleweed and unfortunately very few copies have survived the years. Some 1,700 delinquent notices were sent out and several board members signed a bank note for $5,000 to pay current expenses.

Such was the shockwave surrounding the untimely death of Al Buck that apparently a number of board members ceased to be active. Therefore, it was important when a letter of historical significance dated December 16, 1952 was located in the files. The content of the letter itself is not significant but the letterhead is for it lists the Board of Directors and the Executive Board and is the only complete list of that year that has been located. Officers were as follows:

President   - Roy K. Stovall
First Vice-President   - Carl Brogan
Second Vice-President   - Lois Howsman (1st woman board member)

Vice-President   - Homer Lawrence
Vice-President   - Owen Marron
Vice-President   - G.W. Evans

The following were listed as board members: Jack Ewing, Walter Jones, H.L. Galles, Jack Danglade, A.D. Brownfield, Steve Brock, J.S. Culbertson, Huling Means, Jr., W.C. Kruger, Glenn T. Emmons, Fletcher Bowman, Robert O. Anderson, Joe DiLisio, and Leo Valdes.[14]

Considering the events affecting the Ranch in 1952 and knowing of the troubles yet to be experienced this researcher found it touching to read a short poem attached to the Christmas Greeting from the Ranch that year. It reads as follows:

They say when you are helping a friend in need
By bringing the peace of a selfless deed,
Touching the starlight wing to wing . . .
The tiniest angels begin to sing.

Written by Esther Wood
Boys Ranch, La Joya, N.M. 1952[15]

Within a year after Al Buck's death a special memorial to him was started by seven of his old friends from the Albuquerque Kiwanis Club. The idea was to set aside 400 acres of irrigated ranch land as a "living memorial." It was hoped that through a special program called the "Buck-A-Month Club" the various service clubs of the State could purchase a registered herd of Black Angus cattle for the Ranch. A reality check of the finances at that time revealed that even the $5,000 donated by the Federation of Women's Clubs had already been used for operating expenses.

When Mr. Pragnell was asked by the Board what was wanted at the Ranch he replied:

We want almost everything. We need a hospital—that is the first consideration. If we are thinking in terms of boys, and in terms of the need of putting more boys here we must begin to think in terms of another dormitory unit, recreational equipment and a good recreation program.[16]

Pragnell went on to explain the needs of a good agricultural program. And he stated the well-known fact that most of the difficulties of the past had been due to the lack of finances. In view of the many different needs of the Ranch he recommended the making of definite and concrete plans through a planning board.[17]

Discussion about the school situation for the Ranch boys seemed to favor the boys attending the local school, "inasmuch as it gave them outside contacts, thereby establishing a more democratic way of life among the Ranch boys."[18] Historically, it is interesting to note that at this same meeting Mr. Pragnell mentioned the continued need for a telephone at the Ranch. One positive item of progress that year was the setting up of a library at the Ranch with some 2,000 books. This was done with help through the women of the extension clubs and the State Library Association.

While the records are inconclusive it appears that age and health finally caught up with the remarkable Cecil Pragnell (see Story Two). By March 1953 Lloyd P. Bloodwood, Sr. was the Ranch Manager and his son L.P. Bloodwood, Jr. was in charge of the livestock. His lengthy report to the Board covering the period March 1 – August 1, 1953 left no doubt as to who was in charge. One of his more interesting statistics was the fact that the livestock herd numbered 93 head with 52 of the head at the Magdalena Ranch of "Dub" Evans (by then President of the Board) and 41 head at the Boys Ranch. Additionally there were listed 17 hogs, 28 sheep and 14 horses as well as chickens and rabbits.[19]

There was considerable discussion that spring about the situation at the La Joya School. The Ranch Manager reported that discrimination against the boys was very evident. In July the directors voted to return the boys to La Joya for another year providing the Ranch received a customary transportation allowance. It was reported that the La Joya Superintendent had made a $300 contribution to the Ranch. By August the La Joya Schools placed a young man by the name of Thompson at the Ranch to drive the school bus and to help the boys with their studies. Mr. Thompson was given room and board but it is unclear how long he stayed.

The issue of a "quiet title" land suit on five acres along the northern boundary was explained to the Board. Actually it turned out to be 5.60 acres and it became a part of the pasture for the Buck Foundation.

Considerable discussions were held that spring concerning unpaid bills and the past-due conservancy liens. In fact the possibility of mortgaging the Ranch was seriously considered because by May 1953 the indebtedness stood at some $37,000. Arthur Praeger, representing a group of Albuquerque businessmen, told the directors that they would continue to support the Ranch but that they wanted to see a statement of finances as well as a plan for the future. To this end Edward P. Ancona of Albuquerque was hired to make a complete analysis of the Ranch and to make recommendations.

During the Fall of 1953 a very detailed list composed of the job descriptions, salaries, and duties of every Ranch employee, officers, board members, and standing committees. Considering the details of this six-page document it seems logical to say that this was the Ranch's first policy manual and it dealt with everything from discipline to the laundress.

By late fall the Board approved a fund raising campaign not to exceed $500,000. It appears that the Ranch's obligations were lowered considerably by the cancellation of several creditors including the following: Rio Grande Steel (Al Buck's former company), the Al Buck Estate, and Powell Electric Company. Occasionally the indebtedness would get nasty. Such as when the Socorro businessman went to court and sued the Ranch for $1,113.41 on an overdue bill. Usually, through the good will of people such as Holm Bursum, Dub Evans, and Buzz Jones, things were quietly worked out.

Fifteen thousand Christmas letters were sent out for 1953 by the Ward Hicks Advertising Company. Holm Bursum told the last gathering of the year that "The only thing needed was to get busy and raise money to pay those obligations."[20] Obviously he was correct for by January it was reported that the Ranch's liabilities had been decreased from $50,000 to approximately $16,000.[21] The newly installed system of having county committees appeared to be working. Both Chavez and Curry Counties were singled out for the successful work of their committees.

It was at the January board meeting that mention was first made of an estate being willed to the Ranch. Records indicate that Mr. William P. Clark of Hobbs had been murdered and that he had left one fourth of his estate to the Boys Ranch. The probation of his will which was to have a tremendous effect on the Ranch dragged on until 1959 and will be explained later.

By late January of 1954 the 38 head of Black Angus cattle bought by the Buck Foundation were at the Ranch and 400 acres of land, both pasture and cropland, were set aside for the care of these animals. Dwight Houston (see Story Four) the agricultural teacher at Ft. Sumner High School became the new Superintendent at the Ranch. Houston proceeded to set up a special program for pigs and lambs, but may be best remembered for selling off all the old junked cars and buses that had been accumulated at the Ranch.

By April, in a search for statewide funding, the Board hired Lee Murphy of Denver, at a salary of $400 per month plus expenses, to visit all of the towns and counties across the state. There is not one shred of evidence as to how long he held this position or what the final results were of the pledge campaign. Apparently, finances had gone from bad to worse for in a letter dated June 5, 1954 all board members were being urged to attend an emergency meeting to be held between the Boys Ranch and the New Mexico Baptist Convention. At that meeting the financial situation of the Ranch was called a "serious predicament" and a "financial crisis." At this time a formal proposal was made by the New Mexico Baptist Convention, "to pay all the indebtedness of the New Mexico Boys Ranch, and to assume the operation of the New Mexico Boys Ranch, hence forth on the basis of which it had been operated in the past. The Convention will take title to the southerly land abutting on Highway 60 and erect there a Baptist Orphanage."[22] The orphanage never came but Walker Hubbard did.

Story One: DUB UNDERWOOD

"Dub" Underwood was born in Abilene, Texas in 1912. As the son of a Baptist minister he grew up in many towns, graduated from high school in Albany, Texas and went on to college at Texas Tech in Lubbock. Graduating in 1933 as an engineer, he moved to Albuquerque in 1936. Following a stint in the U.S. Navy during World War II, in which he served as a gunnery officer, Underwood started his own construction company. One of his friends in the Albuquerque Kiwanis Club was Al Buck the founder of the Boys Ranch.

Author: How did you get a name like "Dub"?

Underwood: The kids in school nicknamed me "Dub" which was the custom in Texas at that time. My formal name is Wyatt but no one knows that.

Author: Did your first job bring you to New Mexico?

Underwood: No, my first job was with the Texas highway department for three years. This was the middle of the Depression and jobs were few. Later I went to work for Truscon Steel which was absorbed by Republic Steel. When they opened a branch in Albuquerque I came here for what was to be three months. I've been here ever since and that was 1936. . . . Albuquerque was about thirty five thousand and where we are sitting was all prairie.

Author: How did you get involved with the Boys Ranch?

Underwood: I was in the Albuquerque Kiwanis Club in the fifties and Al Buck, who started the Boys Ranch, was one of the big members. He was the owner of a steel fabricating plant. In fact when we first came out here Al was a dealer for our steel company in stock steel products that we sold through local firms. Mr. Buck was the second man I met in Albuquerque. Buck conceived of the idea (of a Boys Ranch) along with three or four other businessmen such as Owen Marron, Bob Tinnin, "Buzz" Jones who is Al's brother-in-law and others. About 1950 I made one or two trips down to the Ranch with some of the Kiwanis to determine some of their needs and what we could do to help. Being in the construction business I thought that I could scrounge enough free work and materials to build a building. We got an architect to draw up the plans. He was also a member of the Kiwanis Club, Dick Milner. Dick drew

up plans for what was to be a sick bay (infirmary), the
office, and quarters for the manager of the Ranch.
We got the building started and the walls up all with
donated materials and labor. We got the bricklayers
union and carpenters union and such to donate labor
on weekends. When they didn't have work some of
them even went down during the week. The only expense to the Ranch was the travel. Three or four went
down in one car. It didn't cost much—gas was forty
cents a gallon. We were going to put a radiant heating
system which at that time was installed with all steel
pipes.

Well, about the time we got ready for this we had one
of the largest steel strikes in the nation's history. Nobody was about to give away anything that had steel in
it. So the building just sat there with the roof deck on, it
didn't even have a roof. It sat for two or three years because when you come to a standstill interest wanes and
it is hard to get going. In two or three years about the
time that I was elected to the Board of Directors we did
get enough money to put the roof on.

Author: Is it true that by 1953-54 the Ranch was in pretty
               serious financial trouble?

Underwood: Yes, the "conservancy taxes" had not been paid, as well
               as the taxes on the land. When the land was acquired it
               was understood from the state (apparently a verbal
               agreement for there is nothing in writing) that the "con-
               servancy taxes" were forgiven. The state sold a lot of
               land throughout the valley that way and I think most of
               it had the same surprise, because the Conservancy Dis-
               trict went to the district court and finally were con-
               firmed that they did have the rights to collect their back
               assessments or take over the land. It's my understand-
               ing that they did repossess quite a bit of acreage.

Author: It is my understanding that something like $50,000 was owed. Is that right?

Underwood: That's the figure that was in my mind, something like $50,000. I think it was more than that and the Conservancy Board agreed to accept $50,000 provided we pay it off within two or three years. This was quite a shock. We had cleaned up much of the indebtedness and then we got hit with this $50,000 which in 1953 or '54 was a considerable amount of money. It was equal at least to half a million dollars today. We had got to the point where we could see daylight and then this hit us and the roof kind of caved in.

. . . I have to give Holm Bursum a lot of credit. Being a banker, a large property owner and from a political family with much support in New Mexico. He was able to pull strings, pull things together, and buy time for us. That really was the salvation at that critical time. Without Holm I doubt that we would have lasted. He knew how to approach people and how to get things done. I have an idea that Holm put in a considerable amount of finances and personal gifts that most of us know nothing about.[23]

Story Two: CECIL PRAGNELL

Cecil Pragnell was one of those early "founding fathers" of the Boys Ranch. His name appears in virtually every set of minutes from the inception of the Ranch. While most people in New Mexico knew him as the Bernalillo County Agricultural Agent who was an expert both in the field of agriculture and in organization work few people knew of his unique background.

At the age of eight young Cecil accompanied his father, a noted Botanist, on an expedition to Africa where in the process of collecting specimens they ended up fighting off a group of pygmies. Later he became the Court Gardener for King Edward VI. Then at age 18 he joined Baden Powell's original group of Boy Scouts. He fought in the Boer War in South Africa; traveled on botanical expeditions to the corners of the world; and in 1940-41 was in charge of the Orchid Display at the World's Fair in San Francisco. He became friends with Al Buck and in early 1951 at the age of 69 he attempted bringing some order to the Ranch itself as he took over the management.

Story Three: JOHN L. HOLMBACH

John Loumen Holmbach was born in Wemberly, Texas on July 3, 1936. His father was an itinerant farm laborer and the family moved around a lot in Texas. During World War II they moved to California where his father worked in the shipyards. For some unexplained reason they then moved to the grandfathers farm in the Ozarks of Arkansas. Here the father abandoned the family of four children and John's mother was forced on to welfare to make ends meet. Soon the family moved again, this time to Carlsbad to be with the mother's sister who had nine children.

Sympathetic teachers in Carlsbad showed John a booklet about the Boys Ranch and asked if he would like to go there. It was during eighth grade that John moved to the Ranch where he stayed for a year-and-a-half. When the Barbers, a dorm parent family left the Ranch and moved in to Belen John went with them as almost an adopted son. Following a stint in the United States Marines John entered the University of New Mexico. Graduating in 1963 with a teaching degree John Holmbach may well be the first college graduate of the Ranch.

The following excerpts are taken from an interview with John after years of teaching in Grand Junction, Colorado. They provide us with a boy's view of the Ranch in the early 1950s.

Author: What did the Ranch look like when you arrived in April of 1951?

Holmbach: Desert. Dry. Sagebrush. Wasn't much there. They had three little quonset huts, one of them was a dairy barn. I milked cows on it. One was used by Toye and Frances Shaddy. We called them Aunt and Uncle and the Wilkeys we called Mom and Pop. We all lived in one dormitory and it still smelled like paint so it hadn't been there very long. Up on the hill was the kitchen and dining room so we walked up there to eat . . . I was boy number thirty-one. That number was on our clothes . . . We went to school at La Joya on the old yellow school bus, later we got a white one.

Author: How did the Ranch kids get along at school?

Holmbach: Oh, they kind of tolerated us, I guess, they were all Spanish speaking. I only had one fight.

Author: What else do you remember about the Ranch?

Holmbach: When we did the milking it was by hand until we got a milking machine. We drank the raw milk. I got to take care of the big old Clydesdale stallion. My job was to feed and water him. He was a big old dude. We had pigs and a sheep. They (the sheep) would get out onto that highway going to Mountain Air and we would have to ride out and find them. We had chickens up on the hill and down very close to the river. I helped to stack the hay and I worked with Shorty.

Author: You mean "Señor Shorty" Ulibarri, right?

Holmbach: Yes, I remember at the eighth grade graduation at La Joya they pronounced my whole name, John Loumen Holmbach. His daughter Sally was in my class so he was there. From there after he would call me John Lumia Holmbach. He didn't pronounce it properly but I guess the name just stuck with him.

Author: Do you remember other people that were there? Managers? Or cooks?

Holmbach: The Wilkeys, before they came to the Ranch, ran the White
Way Cafe in Belen and when they came to the Ranch they
brought their cook, Ruth, with them. When I came back
from the Marines to visit the Barbers they were back in
Belen running the White Way Cafe. The Barbers were
only at the Ranch for a short while.

Author: **Have you kept track of any of the boys that were with
you at that time?**

Holmbach: No, I have not. But one time in Japan I ran across Merrill
Marshall (another boy). He was in the Navy and I was in
the Marines. He was a cute kid, a real ladies' man with
the girls at La Joya. He is the only one that I ever came
across in all the years and I only talked to him for a few
minutes and then he was gone.

. . . by the way, I was at the Ranch when we went down to
Truth or Consequences and took part in the ceremony that
changed the name over from Hot Springs. And one of our
boys was involved in the radio show with Ralph Edwards,
at that time. We had a sheriff's posse (organized by Roy
Stovall who took Al Buck's position when Buck was
killed. Stovall headed the Sierra County Sheriff's Posse)
and we rode in the parade with Governor Ed Mechem.

Author: **Any other stories or anything particular you remember?**

Holmbach: Yeah, I have a scar on my chest from the Ranch. I had a
brand new yellow T-shirt on. Somebody had donated it
and was brand new. We were running around the barn
one night and ran full tilt into that barbed wire fence.
Ruined my brand new yellow t-shirt.

If you were to ask me, did the Ranch have a positive effect
on me, I'm sure it did but there is no way of measuring it,
because there's no way of knowing where I would have
gone. I am sure that I would never have made college and

that I would never have been a school teacher. I'm sure that would never have transpired. I probably would have been quite a bit like my dad was, you know, just hit and miss jobs.

Author: Do you think that they instilled some good moral values in you?

Holmbach: The biggest thing it did to me is to let me know that there is another way of life than what I was in. That there was something out there that I could obtain, a way of life that was different. It opened my eyes to the world.[24]

Story Four: DWIGHT and GRACE HOUSTON

Dwight O. Houston was born in Randlett, Oklahoma, across the river from Burkburnett, Texas on October 6, 1913. He was a graduate of Oklahoma State University and prior to his arrival at the Boys Ranch he taught agriculture at Ft. Sumner High School in Eastern New Mexico. Grace was born in Davis, Oklahoma on October 22, 1919. She graduated from Reydon High School and the Mid Continent Business College in Oklahoma City.

The Houstons were at the Ranch for a year-and-a-half beginning in February 1954. Their memories are an insightful view of those very difficult days. They left the Ranch primarily because they had three teenage daughters and with thirty-six boys they found life getting out of hand.

Author: What work did the boys do in those days?

Dwight: Well, they had to do all the work around the Ranch. We were short of money in those days and couldn't take them on trips like they do now. They did all the work except cook. My wife eventually was the cook. There were twenty-one or twenty-two head of registered Angus (the Al Buck Memorial herd) and three or four milk cows. They had gotten rid of the horses with money so tight.

Author: **Did you have farm machinery?**

Dwight: That was a big problem. The guy before me (Cecil Pragnell)
. . . Now this is going to be critical, I don't mean it to be
that way, but it was what we had to overcome, he went out
and bought a three thousand dollar automatic baler. String-
tie, everything was automatic, so all you needed was one
boy to pull it. For eleven-twelve hundred he could have
bought a wire-tie baler and more boys could have been put
to work. This automatic baler hadn't been perfected and it
was always broke down. The boys had nothing to do and
you couldn't keep this thing running.

Author: **Mrs. Houston, what did you do while Dwight managed
the   Ranch?**

Grace: Be easier to tell you what I didn't do, I think! I was in
charge of the cooking, the laundry, the cleaning of the one
dormitory (there were two) and supervising the other.
Dwight spent so much time in Albuquerque, getting supplies and food and we were talking about begging, and I
was in charge while he was gone, I'd have to drive the
school bus if he wasn't there. The boys helped me in the
kitchen. We were up at six o'clock in the morning as we
went to bed at nine o'clock in the evening. Some of the
churches in Belen would bring homemade pies or homemade cakes down almost every Sunday for the boys.

Author: **Did you bake your own bread?**

Dwight: We had a deal with Meade's Bread in Albuquerque. Every
Monday morning, I'd crank up that old International truck
we had and head for Meade's. All the bread that they picked
up Monday morning, you know that wasn't sold over the
weekend, that was given to us. Great big cardboard boxes

were put in our cooler-refrigerator at the Ranch and kept there all week. We'd have enough bread to last the whole week. Never any mold or mildew.

Author: **Did you raise much of your food or swap crops?**

Dwight: No, we didn't raise anything. Most of that that was under irrigation had been allowed to alkali out. Black alkali they called it and the only thing that growed on it was a type of salt grass because it was so heavy in alkali. The rain water wouldn't penetrate two inches so very little grass was grown on it. We raised some chili down by the river. When I went there we didn't have any, didn't have the money to buy it, so when we finally got to growing our own chili, it was available to the boys. They even put it on their hot cakes.

Author: **Now, wait a minute. I've never heard of anybody putting chili on hot cakes!**

Dwight: Well, that's how bad it was, they were craving it. They were craving it. You do get a craving for chili . . . (for the author who does love chili this was just too much!).

Author: **Mrs. Houston, do you recall any stories about the boys' background? Where they come from, et cetera.**

Grace: Yes, there is one story I can tell you but I get kind of emotional when I tell it. Jose, at that time was the only boy from out of state. He was from El Paso, Texas and he helped me in the kitchen. One time he wanted to know why we acted like we loved our girls so much. I said, "Jose, where did you come from? Where are your folks?" And he said, "I don't really know." Then he said, "You know, Mom, the last time I remember seeing my mother and daddy was at that corner down in El Paso where they have the stoplights. And there's a tall building and they gave me some money and told me to go in and get some candy and when I got

my candy, they'd be back around and pick me up. And I
haven't seen them since."

Jose was loose in El Paso for five years. I said "Jose, where
did you stay?" And he said, "There's two tall buildings
about a foot or so apart and I slept between those buildings
in an old bathtub." I said, "Where did you get your clothes
and what did you eat?" "Oh," he said, "it's real easy, you
know to take clothes off a clothesline because lots of people's
leaves their clothes out overnight." Then he said, "But I
can tell you one thing, Mom, I never did take anything
from anybody that needed it worse than I did."

[Author's note: Jose was twelve or thirteen when he came
to the Ranch. He had been abandoned on the streets of El
Paso at age seven or eight.]

Author: Dwight, are there any humorous stories that you could
           share with us?

Dwight: Well, when I first went to the Ranch my family was still
           living over in Fort Sumner. I'd go over on Saturday night
           and came back late Sunday or Monday morning. Well, one
           Monday I pulled down to the yard and I saw one of the kids
           sneaking around the barn. The school bus had already gone
           and these boys had hid out and missed the bus. I said to
           one of the men, "Get them in my car, take them up the
           highway and kick them out and make them walk every foot
           of that to school!" (It's about three miles). He did that once
           and when they got out they cut through a field and fence
           and went down on the Rio Grande. He chased them and
           finally got them back in the car and brought them back to
           the Ranch. He said, "What'll I do now?" I said, "Take them
           down to the road again, and kick them out, follow along,
           and see that they walk every foot of it." And they did and I
           never had another kid miss the bus.[25]

NOTES:

1. Fourth Annual Meeting, January 30, 1950.
2. Ibid.
3. Ibid.
4. Ibid p.7.
5. Meeting of the Executive Committee, March 27, 1950.
6. Minutes of the Education and Recreation Committee, May 21, 1950.
7. Committee on Admissions, August 2, 1950.
8. Board of Admission Records, October 16, 1950.
9. Letter to Al Buck quoted in the Executive Minutes, January 3, 1951.
10. Meeting of the Directors and Advisors, April 1, 1951.
11. Ibid.
12. Ibid.
13. Committee on Admissions report February 11, 1952, N.M.B.R. files.
14. Boys Ranch files 1952.
15. Ibid.
16. Minutes Meeting Board of Directors, February 17, 1952.
17. Ibid.
18. Ibid.
19. Report of the Manager to the Officers and Directors, March 1 – August 1, 1953.
20. Board of Directors Meeting, December 4, 1953.
21. Board of Directors Meeting, December 4, 1953.
22. Letter to the Directors and Executive Vice-Presidents N.M.B.R. files, June 5, 1954.
23. Interview with Dub Underwood, June 26, 1991, Albuquerque, New Mexico.
24. Interview with John L. Holmbach, June 20, 1992, Grand Junction, Colorado.
25. Interview with Dwight and Grace Houston, June 20, 1991, Hurley, New Mexico.

Chapter Four
THE WALKER HUBBARD ERA

For many Americans 1954 is best remembered for the nationally televised hearings of Senator Joseph R. McCarthy and his communist witch hunt. At the same time numerous New Mexicans remember that as the year J. Robert Oppenheimer, of Los Alamos fame, was dismissed from government service. For the Boys Ranch 1954 marks the beginning of a new era. In a meeting held at the Hilton Hotel in Albuquerque on July 26, 1954 and with fourteen of the twenty directors present a new set of officers was unanimously elected. They were as follows:

President	- Holm Bursum (Socorro)
Vice-President	- J.W. Wilfreth (Springer)
Secretary	- Lewis Myers (Albuquerque)
Treasurer	- Carter Waid (Belen)
Executive Officer	- Superintendent Walker Hubbard (Portales)

This new Board represented the new Baptist influence. Lewis A. Myers was at this time the Editor-Manager of the Baptist New Mexican newspaper. Carter Waid was the owner of the newspaper in Belen and was a member of the Baptist Board. Walker Hubbard was the Superintendent of the Baptist Children's Home at Portales. Also present at the meeting was Dr. Harry P. Stagg the President of the New Mexico Baptist Convention. (See Story One and Story Two.)

At this historic reorganizational meeting the new Superintendent, Walker Hubbard, outlined his plans for an immediate finance campaign. Letters were to be sent to all state residents whose personal worth exceeded $50,000 and the Baptist Children's Home loaned the Boys Ranch $1,000 immediately for the purpose of meeting "emergency bills."[1]

Historically, it is interesting to note that at this now famous reorganization meeting a donation was received by Edwin Mechem, Sr., a Las Cruces attorney and father of the then Governor Edwin Mechem, Jr. In making the gift in memory of his son Jesse, who lost his life in World War II, the donor lamented that New Mexicans, "are not fully aware of the great work carried on by the Boys Ranch for wayward boys."[2]

By September news of the Boys Ranch began appearing regularly in the Baptist New Mexican newspaper. The first editorial written about the Ranch informed its readers about the background. Stating that, "when in the process of administration, the institution, primarily supported by a restricted few in the service clubs of Albuquerque and other scattered cities, came to the point of financial stress, the Board of Directors turned to our Baptist folk with an S.O.S."[3] Thus, a new Board was formed.

It is obvious that the new arrangement was good for the Ranch. In fact, it probably saved the Ranch from being mortgaged or even sold. At the annual meeting in January 1955, Superintendent Hubbard reported that the indebtedness, which was around $48,500 when the present Board took over last July 28th, had been reduced to approximately $28,000.[4] It was at this same meeting that it was agreed that Hubbard's salary would be divided equally between the Ranch and the Baptist Convention. The Superintendent was to remain living in Portales and a gas, oil, car allowance of $25 per month was provided. Some $25,000 worth of physical improvements were made to the Ranch in the first six months, including the completion of the headquarters-dormitory which was to accommodate fourteen more boys. The budget for 1955 was set at $47,141 with specified financial quotas being set for each of the 32 counties in the state.[5]

Things were looking up for the Ranch. On a motion by J.R. Brown of Las Vegas and seconded by Merle Tucker of Gallup an announcement was made to the press that, "under no circumstance that can be foreseen at this time will the Boys Ranch be for sale, nor would any move to have the Ranch taken over by the state be looked upon with any favor whatsoever."[6] Even the barren Ranch grounds, which had been pretty bleak, improved. An article in the Baptist New Mexican complimented the Fruit Avenue Church of Albuquerque for providing six spreading junipers as wind breakers. The article stated that, "this gift follows an appeal, primarily through secular organizations and individual

businesses, for help in a landscaping plan touching fully ten acres of
the immediate dormitory grounds. The project is already virtually
completed."[7]

Having three teenage daughters living among the two dozen neglected and delinquent boys was a little too much responsibility for the
Houstons who departed in May of 1955. They were replaced by Mr. &
Mrs. J.V. Starkey. Starkey was an experienced worker in the Boy Scout
movement and had been employed at the Children's Home in Portales.
By all accounts the Starkeys were excellent workers and satisfactory in
every way. Their resignation on March 17, 1957 was due to the poor
health of Mrs. Starkey. They were replaced by Mr. & Mrs. Marvin
McSmith. McSmith had been reared in Socorro, was a UNM graduate in
1953 and had been a football coach at Mountainair and Eunice. Mrs.
McSmith replaced Mrs. Starkey as one of the housemothers at the
Ranch.[8]

In January 1956 the Board elected its next set of officers. Elected
were:

President   - Holm Bursum, Socorro
Vice-President   - Dr. Floyd Golden, Portales
Secretary   - Editor Lewis A. Myers, Albuquerque
Treasurer   - W.A. Sutter, Clovis
and "that unmatched guide of youth":
Superintendent. - Walker Hubbard, Portales

These minutes are the first mention of both Andy Sutter of Clovis and
J.B. Tidwell of Hobbs. Both men proceeded to devote many years to the
work of the Boys Ranch. It was reported at this time that the Ranch had
operated during 1955 on a budget of $40,179.64 with a total of 31 boys
for a per capital cost of about $1,200. The new budget of $52,000 was
presented by the Superintendent and adopted by the Board. This budget
was broken down by counties and allocations. The largest contributors
for several years were Bernalillo, Dona Anna, Lea, Chavez, Curry, Eddy,
Roosevelt, and Santa Fe counties.[9]

It was reported at this meeting that the Buck Memorial Foundation
cattle herd of forty-five cows had been transferred to the Ranch for
$5,700, which was repayable at $1,400 annually. Eventually, this trans-
fer totalled out at $6,500. Jennie Culberson and Lanarsh Coward of the

State Cosmetologist Association were introduced to the Board as guests. For years this organization conducted statewide drives for the Ranch including a "Boys Ranch Day" on the streets of Albuquerque. On at least one occasion Ranch boys participated and over $800 was raised in nickels and dimes. The meeting concluded with this optimistic statement:

> The attitude of praise prevailed and the spirit of the Board was generally shown in the unanimous passing of many motions and visioned adoption of advanced plans for the future.[10]

It must have been obvious to all that the Boys Ranch had entered a new era.

The phraseology of Editor Lewis Myers is reflected in the January 27, 1957 meeting which reads:

> The waters were placid and all sails were set in the same direction. The fellowship was, therefore, wholesome and the actions taken were visioned and constructive.[11]

Actually, there was both good news and bad news to report. The good news was that a one-half gift proposition on a house in Truth or Consequences was expected to net the Ranch around $5,000. The bad news was that the pesky "conservancy tax" issue was still casting its shadow over the Ranch.

The subject of "surplus commodities" is reported on at this gathering. In the past some surplus articles such as army beds had been received, however, this is the first mention of surplus food. Dr. Golden from Portales reported on great success in obtaining beans, rice, lard, cheese, meal, dried milk, canned beef, etc.[12]

Superintendent Hubbard called a special meeting of the Executive Board on April 10th to study a unique offer. A hunting club from Albuquerque was interested in building and leasing a duck lake on Ranch property near the river. After several meetings an agreement was reached which included the stipulation that no drinking would ever be tolerated on Ranch property. A dike and a dam were actually built and paid for by the club members with the following result:

> With the first trickle of water, decoys were planted and

posted signs were erected by the hunters, but the pond has
remained, in the main, a dry gulch.[13]

By this time a note had been made at the Albuquerque National
Bank for money to pay off all indebtedness on the Ranch. Creditors were
being asked to reduce the amounts due them as a contribution to public
welfare. The Board hoped that no less than 20 percent would be granted.
For the record, it must be stated there was unanimity in the insistence
that every dollar would be paid, even without reduction, if the creditor
insisted. Andy Sutter of Clovis replaced Carter Waid as the Board
Treasurer. Mrs. Ruth Alexander of Santa Fe and Mrs. Lucille Green of
Hobbs joined the Board of Directors, with Mrs. Green serving as 2nd
Vice-President.[14]

Walker Hubbard's Christmas plea for funds that year (1957)
mentioned the purchase of a new sixty-four passenger school bus which
had cost $4,000; a cottage remodeled to provide an extra bedroom; a
living room added to one cottage; and extensive repairs to a large
bathroom. Hubbard's statistics show a total of 52 boys were cared for
throughout the year. Of these nineteen were released to relatives, two
went into foster homes and two entered the military. The year ended
with 29 boys living at the Ranch, of which eight were from Santa Fe
County and six were from Bernalillo County (Albuquerque). Thirteen
other New Mexican counties and El Paso, Texas were represented.[15]

On January 4, 1958 the following officers were elected:

President   - Holm Bursum [reelected] he was also serving as
                    the President of the First Bank of Socorro
Vice-President - Dr. Floyd Golden, Portales [reelected]
Secretary   - Carl Brogan, Albuquerque
                    [replaced Lewis A. Myers]
Treasurer   - Andy Sutter, Clovis [reelected]

Other officers of the corporation that year included:

Ollie Dennis (T or C)   Carter Waid (Belen)
Dub Underwood (Albuquerque)   Merle Tucker (Gallup)
G.W. Evans, (Magdalena)   J.B. Tidwell (Hobbs)
Ruth Laughlin Alexander (Santa Fe) J.W. Wilfreth (Springer)
Tom Brown (Artesia)   J.B. Brown, Sr. (Las Vegas)

Ben Archer (Hatch)   Jess May (Farmington)
Harry Latham (Deming)   Billy Holder (Alamogordo).[16]

At that meeting McSmith, the resident manager, reported that the Ranch livestock included 6 horses, 20 hogs, and 87 cows—including 6 milk cows. The Treasurer, Andy Sutter, revealed a "healthy financial condition"[17] indicating most of the counties had raised their allocation of the budget. Once again the issue of the back "conservancy taxes" entered the discussion, but without a solution.[18]

It is obvious that a great deal of hard work had been accomplished during the year of 1958. A careful reading of the Progress Report (January 1958 to January 1959) reveals, among other things, the following: 41.9 acres of land re-leveled, 75 acres of new hay, 1,434 feet of underground irrigation pipeline installed, lawns and 27 rose bushes planted, a new swimming pool completed, all buildings repainted and repaired, 100 trees planted, forty acres of new land to be farmed, all fences rebuilt, etc. But the statement which is most revealing concerning the new direction of the Ranch is the following:

> The thing most proud of is the fact that the reputation of all boys is above average in school, church, and the boys are now welcome anywhere we take them. All boys have brought grades up at least one level. The boys now take pride in the fact that they are from the New Mexico Boys Ranch.[19]

Many people associate the year 1959 with Fidel Castro and the culmination of the Cuban Revolution. However, for our topic it is far more interesting to reflect on the popular songs that America was singing that year. Three of those songs, "He's Got the Whole World In His Hands," "Everything's Coming Up Roses," and "High Hopes" sure were appropriate.

Today the minutes of January 26, 1959 need to be etched in gold leaf or at the very least placed in a special file folder because that was the date when J.B. Tidwell announced the news that the Clark Estate had been settled. The New Mexican Boys Ranch received a total of $88,070.18, this being twenty-five percent of four properties sold in Hobbs. Tidwell stated that $5,000 was being held back for taxes and other obligations and that some of the oil leases might bring an additional profit at a future date.[20]

To this day it remains somewhat of a mystery as to who the person was that influenced Mr. Clark to include the Boys Ranch in his will. It is frequently said in various religious circles that "God moves in mysterious ways" and this was one of those occasions.

The last note owed by the Ranch was brought to the Board being stamped "PAID" 1/14/59 and was in the amount of $9,000. The Board was unanimous in asking that it be kept in the files as a reminder of trials during the last four years.[21]

On a motion by Underwood and seconded by Evans the Board established a new Advisory Council. This was to be composed of one member from each county and their duty was to assist the Ranch Board, but without voting privileges. Lewis Myers, who had resigned in January 1958 due to ill health, was returned to the Board and new members Tom Wiley (Santa Fe) and Chancy Snyder (Silver City) were elected. It is interesting to note that due to their tremendous interest in the Ranch the Cosmetologist Association was awarded a place on the Board with the Executive Committee naming the person. Following the meeting special letters of appreciation for their contributions were sent to Jack Howard of Rainbow Bread, The Kiwanis Club of Albuquerque, and the Bishop Printing Company of Portales.

From time to time various items, money, and real estate have been left in wills to the Boys Ranch. In 1959 one of the more unique items was contained in the Estate of Catherine M. O'Dell. Mrs. O'Dell was a former teacher in the Albuquerque Public Schools and was at one time the executive secretary of the Albuquerque Civic Council. Her husband, Clyde, was a one-half blood Osage Indian from Oklahoma. Clyde and Catherine had attended the University of Oklahoma at the same time and both moved to Albuquerque for their health about 1930. Clyde predeceased Catherine and left her his mineral rights which in turn she left to the Boys Ranch at the suggestion of her attorney. The oil rights had produced $2,085 of income the year before and their estimated value was $17,500.[22]

As of December 31, 1959 the estimated value of the New Mexico Boys Ranch was $328,120. This figure is broken down in a report that lists the following: land - $129,500; buildings - $134,000 (3 dormitories are listed); equipment - $44,155; livestock - $14,015; and vehicles - $6,450. The same report estimated the Ranch provided $4,800 worth of their own needs such as chickens, milk, beef and hay. Of the fifty-eight boys who went through the Ranch during 1959 fourteen were from Bernalillo County with fourteen other counties being represented. Proudly listed at the top of this report is the fact that two of the boys had entered college.[23]

During the annual meeting held on January 25, 1960 Superintendent Hubbard discussed an issue being pressed by the La Joya Public Schools. The fact was that while the boys had actually changed schools to Belen the year before there continued to be a rivalry between the districts. The directors voted, "their desire for the Ranch boys to have the educational opportunities provided by the Belen Public School.[24] At issue, among other things, were transportation funds provided by the state. Statistics presented at the meeting showed a total of 131,647 letters had been mailed out to donors during the year with a total net return of $46,359.92.[25]

> The progress Report for 1960 included these listed honors: Out of 13 entrees at Valencia County Junior Livestock Show our boys placed 12 animals . . . 1 Reserve Champion . . . 3 First Place awards.

> Out of 13 entrees at Socorro Junior Livestock Show and County Fair our boys placed 13 animals . . . 2 Grand Champions . . . 1 Reserve Champion . . . 4 First Place awards . . . 1 Herdsman Trophy won by Art Crespin.

> Out of 2 entrees at State Fair our boys placed one 2nd Place and one 3rd Place.

> One of our boys took 2nd Place at the New Mexico Golden Gloves regional tournament in Albuquerque.

> Boys Ranch 7 man boxing team won 5 trophies - 2 Champion - 3 Runner-up at Grants Boxing Tournament - weights range from 85 to 123 pounders.

> Two boys consistently on the honor roll in school.

> Five boys placed in special chorus in school.[26]

By 1961 it was obvious the work of the Board of Directors required more than an "annual meeting: so a July date was added. A "Cattlemen's Day" at the Ranch was established and was to be preceding the opening of the State Fair. By means of a special program and a barbecue all of the state's ranchers were to be honored. The next year the title was changed to "Stockman's Day." This was an annual event at the Ranch for several years until it was dropped due to the small number of ranchers attending. However, calves continued to arrive from these ranchers with 70 coming in 1963 alone.

By mid year the ugly subject of the "conservancy tax" payments was once again raised. This time the Executive Committee explored the possibility of selling off at least some of the land that was under the "conservancy tax" (irrigated land). Out of the one page set of minutes for July 14, 1961 comes this startling statement. "Carl Brogan discussed the proposed sale of property, mentioning that the property had been offered for $450,000 with a down payment of $150,000 and the remainder to be paid in yearly payments of $20,000. Motion was made, seconded and carried for the committee to continue negotiations with this matter."[27]

In October Walker Hubbard was busy sending out letters with pleas for money to pay the taxes. One letter survives these bleak days and contains words like:

. . . very serious emergency.
. . . we must have $25,000 immediately.
. . . we do not have this amount of money to make the
         assessment payment.
. . . the fate of the Boys Ranch lies in your hands.[28]

Whatever the sudden pressure was that had prompted the radical move to sell, it must have been quietly resolved for at the next board meeting the proposal was withdrawn. Superintendent Hubbard did explain that "The present conservancy charge is now made only on the land that the Ranch farms. This amounts to $1,107.71 per year. Old assessments were based on all acres under the Conservancy Ditch. In 1961 $15,500.00 was paid on the accumulated conservancy debt and another $10,586.52 was paid by January 1962."[29]

Throughout the years a wide variety of fund raisers were tried, some successful and others quickly dropped. In 1962 a unique arrangement was made between the Boys Ranch and a businessman. Gum and candy machines were purchased by the businessman, placed in various businesses in Albuquerque with 20 percent of the gross income coming to the Ranch who were the official sponsors. No further record is found of this chewy business!

Officers elected for 1963 were:

President   - Dub Evans
1st Vice-President - Holm Bursum
2nd Vice-President - Lucille Green
Secretary   - Carl Brogan
Treasurer   - Andy Sutter

Also attending that meeting were Walker Hubbard, J.B. Brown, Dub Underwood, Harry Lathan, J.B. Tidwell, J.W. Wilfreth, and Chancy Snyder. Finances showed an income of $113,897.69 which was an increase over the previous year. An operating budget of $77,500 for expenses and $25,000 for promotion was accepted. Ranch manager Wayne Britton (see Story Three) made his report stating that some 69 boys had been cared for during this year.

Following the receipt of another property, this one in Portales and the proceeds of which were to be shared with the Children's Home, the Board decided it was time to get professional help. A contract was then made with the firm of Lloyd Wagnon and Associates to provide services in the fields of tax exemptions, wills and bequests for the Ranch.

In a move to help alleviate the financial strain on the Ranch there was an attempt to sell off a portion of the land in 1965. Various letters and notes in the Ranch files indicate a neighbor identified as Weldon Burris of La Joya offered $17,500 for a total of 1,161 acres. One letter states that Burris was negotiating with the new Ranch Manager Barry Morgan (See Story Four). A map in the files indicates that the land being offered was east of Highway #47 as well as land near the San Juan ditch.[30]

By January of 1966 and after much discussion the proposed sale was rejected, but an offer was made to lease Burris a part of the unused land. Provision was made for the State Cowbelles Organization to have a member named by them on the Boys Ranch Board of Directors. The Cowbelles worked hard encouraging ranchers to give calves to the Boys Ranch. A total of 95 calves were donated in 1967 alone, bringing the

Ranch herd up to 144 cows. Statistics presented at the meeting indicate that 69 boys had been cared for during the year. Promotional letters had shown a return of $86,350.49 with a total income of $120,839.56.[31] The following year these same statistics had risen to 72 boys, an income of $122,553.21 and a budget of $137,000 was approved.[32]

Barry Morgan's report for 1967 shows it to be a very active year and provides the reader with an inside look at the boys' achievements. It reveals an active 4-H Club, two First Places (including the Grand Champion), two Third Places, 1 Fifth and Sixth Places at the Socorro County Fair. Gardening produce and flowers also won many ribbons at the fair. Other projects submitted included wildlife, leather craft, first aid and health, woodcraft, tractors and electrical. In all their projects the boys won many ribbons and $34 in prize money. Six boys received awards for their 4-H record books.

A meat cutting class was taught at the Ranch with one young man going to the state meet with his meat cutting demonstration. The boys' basketball team participated in several games and tournaments. The baseball team of staff and boys played in the Belen league and won the Sportsmanship Trophy. During July twenty-five boys attended Boy Scout Camp. A hunter safety course was completed by sixteen boys and some of these were taken on a weekend hunting trip. One boy was on the high school football team, three were in the school operetta and almost all participated in the church Christmas program.

It is interesting to note that Morgan's report also lists former Ranch boys in the service such as Don Vestal in Germany, Art Crespin in the Navy, and Tommy Tucker at Fort Bliss (Army). He concluded his report by stating that 15 former Ranch boys had stopped by to visit.[33]

Lots of good things happened at the Ranch in 1967 such as: a new laundry building, new laundry equipment, a new twelve-passenger suburban station wagon, new corrals, box car, squeeze chute, and slaughter house were added to the Rodeo Arena. The exterior of the buildings were refinished and the old laundry building was converted into additional hobby shop space.

Of the sixty boys cared for during the year twenty-six were from Bernalillo County with sixteen other counties being represented. It is interesting to note that in the first breakdown of income it was revealed that 78.8 percent came from donations, 10 percent from estate income, 11 percent from farm income and .002 percent from memorial gifts. Including buildings, land, inventories, stock, funds and savings the Boys Ranch was valued at $454,744.40.[34]

In an October 2, 1968 letter to the Ranch donors Walker Hubbard spoke of the cramped and inadequate housing facilities and that an expansion program was vitally needed. He asked the donors to give generously in helping to construct a new cottage to take care of sixteen boys at the cost of $43,000.[35] Of significant importance is the fact that by the end of 1968 the very last of the old conservancy debt was finally paid off.

Throughout the 1960s Hubbard's letters to donors frequently cited the exact names of the boys and their individual case history. Shocking home conditions, fights, abuse, drunkenness, desertion, and general neglect were all too common. The following are excerpts from some of those stories:

> BILL—12 years old. Parents were both chronic drunkards. Home life was filled with bitter arguments and often drunken brawls. Mother deserted father and son. Bill was placed in a foster home, but could not adjust. He was listed as an unhappy, resentful, disillusioned boy.

> SAMMY—age unlisted. Mother died of an overdose of sleeping tablets. Father refused to take any real responsibility and has denied him affection, encouragement and guidance.

> DAN—13 years old and in constant trouble. Had already spent considerable time in jail and was known by every policeman in town. His juvenile officer wrote to ask the Ranch if they would take him saying, "There is no hope for this boy if he remains in this city."[36]

In one of those real life turn-around stories this last young man graduated from Belen High School. While there he won the "Best Mannered Boy" Award, won a letter in football and was the Novice Heavyweight Golden Gloves Champion in his senior year. Following military duty with the Special Forces in Germany and with a new wife and son Don came back to the Boys Ranch as a houseparent. As Walker

Hubbard wrote in 1971, "Twelve years ago he was part of the problem and today he is part of the solution."[37]

Walker Hubbard sought out sixty substitute parents for the boys at Boys Ranch. He asked these sponsors for $40 per month or $480 per year to assure each boy the best possible chance to know the full values of a wholesome family life environment. He included an unsigned and undated poem which really said it all.

> When a feller's feeling friendly
> Cause he's got a bit ahead,
> And he sees some little feller
> With a heart that feels like lead,
> Ain't it good to have a nest egg
> Tell me, ain't it good to give?[38]

Story One: HARRY P. STAGG

The story of Harry Perkins Stagg is a book by itself and it is called: *Harry P. Stagg: Christian Statesman* (Broadman Press, Nashville, Tennessee, 1976). This book was written by Bonnie Ball O'Brien the wife of Chester O'Brien, former Executive Director of the Baptist Convention of New Mexico and the successor to Dr. Stagg.

Born on October 1, 1898 in a small Louisiana community Harry was the third son of a Baptist preacher. Indeed even his grandfather had been a Baptist minister. During his youth in Louisiana he harbored dreams of becoming a medical missionary and was in school for that purpose when the First World War broke out. Going to New Orleans to enlist he was sent to join up with General Pershing, who was returning from chasing Pancho Villa around Northern Mexico. Stagg became a chapter member of the First Division and was on the first allied ship to land in France.

Author: How long were you in France?

Stagg: Well, I was in France almost two years. My regiment, the 28th Infantry, made the first all-American attack against the

Germans at Cantigny. Incidentally, I was reported killed in action, but that was finally corrected. (Both the author and Dr. Stagg had a good laugh on that one.) Stagg participated in the Second Battle of the Marne where he was wounded. He came home with medical problems that have plagued him throughout the rest of his life.

Author: Tell me about your schooling after WWI?

Stagg: I went to Louisiana College, a Baptist college, and then on t the New Orleans Baptist Bible Institute, which later became New Orleans Baptist Theological Seminary. While in college I was pastor of a little church in Bentley, LA. I was still set on being a medical missionary, but I became very ill. A friend came by from Florida and convinced my family to let me go west with him. I almost died twice before I got to Albuquerque—that was March, 1925.

For thirteen years Stagg served as a pastor in Gallup, frequently rising from his sick bed to preach. Elected to the position of Executive Secretary of the Baptist Convention of New Mexico in 1937 he held that position for a record thirty years. During his tenure church membership grew from 15,000 to 90,000 primarily through his tireless efforts. In the 1950s he learned to fly his own airplane and to this day remains the only New Mexico resident to preach to the annual Southern Baptist Convention.

Joseph B. Underwood, a one-time consultant with the Southern Baptist Convention, wrote this tribute to Harry Stagg:

He *cared*, intensely and personally, for individuals and for churches. He knew how to rejoice with those who rejoiced and how to weep with those who sorrowed. His perceptive mind and heart enabled him to recognize acute problems. His compassion caused him to minister in love. He was one with the Baptists of New Mexico.[39]

It was this care and compassion which lead Dr. Stagg and the Baptist Convention to the Boys Ranch in 1954.

Author: So tell me, how did you get involved with the New Mexico Boys Ranch?

Stagg: When I accepted this position (Executive Secretary) the Convention was bankrupt. It had been five years without an executive leader, with only an official elected as a dollar-a-year man to sign legal papers, that's what I picked up. We were very slow getting things done and it was very difficult to pay old debts and clear things up before advancing a program. We had this orphans' home at Portales and the superintendent and wife were running it (Walker and Dorothy Hubbard).

. . . I was in Rotary and the club secretary was my good friend Carl Brogan. One day at Rotary he called me aside and said, "We are in trouble at Boys Ranch. Looks like we're going to lose it. We need help and your Convention can take this over and save it." I said, "Carl, there's no way in the world we can do that. We are struggling to keep our church home alive." Well, he kept hitting me so I took a look at the record.

. . . When Al Buck died there was no one else in the Kiwanis Club that was willing to take over and that's when the trouble started. We talked it over, had several conferences about it and as I recall there was even a day set for a sheriff's sale. Carl got real serious. Then I talked to Walker Hubbard and his wife and our leading board members of the Convention. They were all interested if there was any way we could help. We met and made them this proposal, which was accepted, that we would help what we could to sustain food and things like that, to save the institution. We would supply our Director of the Children's Home to the Boys Ranch Board for half time without cost. The main thing that I felt really sad about was that Mrs. Hubbard was left half the time to run the Children's Home. They were an unusual and outstanding couple. This proposition was accepted by the Court and the foreclosure stopped.

. . . The second move was to overhaul their Board and they agreed. The whole Board agreed with what we wanted to do and were willing to cooperate. One-third of the Board resigned so we filled that third with new members. The next third resigned and we filled that. The third third resigned and we filled that third. We picked some of those old board members and kept them, the key ones we wanted. Brother Hubbard knew men all over the state so he had a pretty good lineup of men to save this Ranch. He nominated those men and we selected that new Board, with representation of the old Board that knew the history and background.

. . . It recuperated faster than we had hoped. It beat our expectations. Then we found that there was a will estimated to be about three hundred thousand. It was stipulated that the Ranch would have to be operating under its own Board and Charter. We weren't able financially to take it over under any consideration . . . I've been very pleased that Carl Brogan persuaded us to go ahead and help and we didn't say no.[40]

Story Two: CARTER WAID

Born on a farm in southern Oklahoma on July 10, 1911 Carter Waid was one of seven children. Graduating from Fletcher Oklahoma High School in 1928 Carter attended Cameron College in Lawton before entering the newspaper business. Thirteen years with the Lawton Constitution saw him move from a cub reporter to city editor. Those were the tough days of the Depression. As Carter says, "I worked two weeks for nothing, because the guy I was succeeding had two weeks to go before they let him out and they owed him the money. They couldn't pay two salaries so I had to work for nothing for two weeks. Then I worked six weeks for six dollars, nine weeks for nine dollars, and twelve weeks for twelve dollars. After five years I was drawing twenty-five dollars a week. That was 1936."

Author: Were those Dust Bowl days?

Waid: They were, but Lawton was not in the Dust Bowl. It suffered
          some. It kind of turned dark at times like cloudy or smog or
          something like that. The economy was very bad. They had
          bread lines where citizens came by the hundreds and lined
          up for meals in downtown Lawton.

          . . . did you know that the Oklahoma Dust Bowl built
          Bosque Farms near here? Nobody lived there and the gov-
          ernment set aside two thousand acres between Los Lunas and
          Isleta. They transported some sixty dairymen out here to live,
          helped give them a herd and let them have the land for almost
          nothing. When I came here in 1947 the only people living
          there were the dairymen and their families. Today it's a town
          of four thousand or more.

Author: Were you a newspaper man during the war?

Waid: I was until 1944 then I went into the Office of War Informa-
          tion, that was a government propaganda agency. I went to
          New York for a year of training. Well I went to England
          first, then Luxembourg and into Germany with the Army
          occupation. I was a civilian with the Army under Eisenhow-
          er's organization. I put out a newspaper there in Germany
          which didn't have an English writer on the staff, all German.

Author: What brought you to New Mexico?

Waid: If I had an opportunity I knew that I was going to try to get
          a little paper somewhere and be on my own. I bought half
          interest in a little weekly in Belen and a chap from Kansas
          bought the other. Three months later we had enough sense
          to merge them. We called it The News Bulletin. We had a
          hand fed press and folded at night by hand. Later I became
          the sole owner.

Author: Is that how you heard of the Boys Ranch?

Waid: Right, it was in our area. I knew the Ranch and went down there occasionally, but it wasn't a very important part of the community. It had a reputation of trying to take needy boys, but it wasn't getting all the financial backing that it needed. It was pretty hard to raise money for it at the time and when Buck was killed it began to lose ground. The Ranch got so it was almost in bankruptcy and they (The Court) were threatening to close it. They approached The New Mexico Baptist Board to take it over. I happened to be on the Baptist Board when that was done. Harry Stagg was the Executive Secretary of the State Baptist Organization and he asked me to serve as Treasurer. I think he wanted somebody here (Belen) who might meet with the local merchants. The shape we were in we didn't have any credit here in town hardly at all.

Author: What was the condition of the treasury?

Waid: Well, it was mostly in the red. We must have owed forty or fifty thousand dollars. Not all in Belen, but to merchants for various things that they needed. I don't think that all of us realized it at the time, but the old Conservancy District here had property taxes and they hadn't been paid. So when Hubbard took over he had a pretty good chore to take charge of all the things.

   . . . Mostly they just lacked money. The Ranch hadn't been established yet in the public's mind as a viable thing. Today it would be hard to go broke with the reputation it has here in the state.

Author: As a newspaper man were you asked to file stories or publish stories on the Ranch?

Waid: Mostly I did it on my own. If it was of high importance I sent it up to Albuquerque to the Journal or maybe the AP wire service. I know that we had some bad publicity in my paper here in Belen. We tried to report the board meetings and some bad statements came out. Walker (Hubbard) kind of heckled me, but he never clamped down or anything like that.

. . . I was on the Board when Alice King came on. She just has an interest in children like that. Alice was a devout member and never seemed to be assuming anything, just a good participant.

The real faithful ones were Jesse May, Andy Sutter, J.B. Tidwell, Holm Bursum from Socorro, he ran for governor once, a rancher from Magdalena named Evans (Dub), Dub Underwood, Ben Archer from Hatch. Lucille Green from Hobbs was head of the state beauticians and she helped tremendously for several years. Tibo Chavez was never on the Board, but as the District Judge and Senate Majority Leader (and Lieutenant Governor) he was a political power at the time and he was interested in the boys and the Ranch.[41]

Story Three: WAYNE BRITTON

Born in Palestine, Texas on October 18, 1919, Wayne Britton graduated from high school in 1937 and moved to Denton, Texas about 1940. After trying college at Baylor University and North Texas State, World War II intervened. Britton says he spent "three years, ten months and four days as a soldier in Africa and Europe." He graduated from Texas Wesleyan College in 1953 with a major in History. Years later he took his Masters Degree from East Texas State and taught vocational education at the college level for over ten years. Wayne Britton was a Ranch Manager at the Boys Ranch from 1960 to 1964. His interview gives a unique view of the Ranch in those years.

Author: How did you get to the Boys Ranch?

Britton: In 1955 I became the pastor of the Rio Grande Baptist Church in Albuquerque. While there I was also teaching school because the church was very small. During the course of my pastorate about 45 children were given to me to place, not a single one of them from my church. I guess the Lord brought me into contact with Walker Hubbard. He knew of my interest in children and in 1960 offered me a position at the Boys Ranch. After praying about it I figured that's where I needed to be. I was there until the fall of '64. I left because I became very ill and the third doctor told me that if I didn't leave New Mexico I would die. I was allergic to everything in New Mexico, mountain cedars, alfalfa dust, tumbleweeds, cockle burrs, horse hair, everything.

Author: What was life like for you?

Britton: The wife and I lived in the high school building with our three children. My salary was $350 per month and my wife received $100 which was what the houseparents received. Of course we had our room and board, but it was difficult because of low salaries to find competent people. We had some very precious people who were very dedicated, there at the Ranch while I was there.

. . . We had a large number of Hispanic boys, most were Anglos, but we always had several Black boys there. There was no race problem ever at the Ranch.

. . . I expected too much from the youngsters because I feel like the thing that they needed more than anything else was to recognize the fact that they had self worth.

. . . The boys kept books on their animals and when they were sold they paid back the Ranch. The balance was the boy's. We opened a savings account for each boy in his own name.

Author: Did you ever have any girls at the Ranch?

Britton: We had one girl at one time. She was from a family with eight children and her mother was twenty-three years old. There were two sets of twins and a child every year. We

took the older boys and the girl. She was about six and a
member of my family for a while. Later on Mr. Hubbard
took her to the Orphan's Home in Portales.

Author: Did you ever pay the farm bills in produce? (Several northern New Mexico schools such as McCurdy Mission
swapped apples and potatoes for goods and services.)

Britton: We paid all of our doctor bills in hay. Dr. Rivas at Belen was
a very, very good doctor and he had some cattle. Of course,
we grew hay and alfalfa. It went at a dollar a bale.

Author: What about clothes for the boys?

Britton: Most of the clothing was bought from Montgomery Ward.
remember one time going down there and buying over one
hundred pairs of jeans they had on sale. The fact of the matter is that the manager got real mad at me because I was
cleaning him out. We had a great deal of good used clothing
given to us. The fact of the matter is that if it was something
up to date, well, the boys just grabbed for it.

Author: Did you do food preparation?

Britton: Not really. Of course we had freezers. At one time we had
twenty-four lockers down in Socorro with pork in them. We
had a plan worked out with a company in Albuquerque to
take cattle there and they would give me credit for it. As I
needed beef or beef products or anything that they had for
that matter I'd go there and draw it.

. . . We had commodities from the government such as peanut butter, cheese, rolled wheat, and corn meal.

. . . We bought honey from peddlers because of the bees that
were in the tamarack (Tamarisk trees are desert shrubs with
lots of flowers.) The honey that was produced was very
stout, very dark honey. One time I bought several 5-gallon

cans of honey, over sixty pounds, at a very cheap price because he couldn't get rid of it.

Author: Did you do everything?

Britton: I had charge of the Ranch, even going to the post office for the money. I'd take it out and sent it to Mr. Hubbard so he could write thank-you notes to everybody. I know for a fact that there were lots of contributions from a dollar up. It was not unusual at all to receive five-dollar bills. Of course, five dollars bought a whole lot.

Author: Was there an attempt to take these boys to a particular church?

Britton: The boys were required to go to church, but it was a church of their choice. As a result I had very excellent rapport with all the local clergy. Fact of the matter is that I had a standing invitation at the rectory to go in and have dinner with the priest or whoever might be there and they had the same privilege of coming to the Ranch.

Author: Did a lot of people stop at the Ranch?

Britton: I do know that when the land developers scraped off some streets out in the desert people would come from a long way off and try to find their lot. They'd drive out in those sandy areas and get stuck. Of course our boys loved to go out there and help pull them out. One time some folks from Washington came . . . and bless the lady's heart, when they got to the Ranch it was just before noon, she had real high heels on, and she walked across that desert in the sand and climbed two or three barbed wire fences. She was in pitiful shape. We brought them in and they had a meal with us and after lunch the boys took our tractor and pulled them out of the sand. When he got back home he sent us a very sizable check.

Author: Did the boys' parents visit? Or did the boys go home for
        vacations?

Britton: Yes, sometimes. We had one youngster who came to us at
        about fifteen, but he was the size of an eight year old. He was
        dwarfed and didn't weigh but about seventy-five pounds,
        very thin. His parents had died and his grandmother raised
        him. When she died there were no other relatives, but he
        wanted to go to the funeral. We tried to teach the boys that
        the New Mexican Highway Patrol was their friends. When
        one was in the area we'd invite them in to have dinner with
        us and they did many times. When there was a need they
        would ferry the youngster the distance of their territory and
        meet another car and they'd ferry them up. We sent Joe home
        that way and he came back the same way. I'm just very, very
        pleased that the Ranch business has expanded to the areas
        where it is now and I rejoice for those who have been res-
        ponsible for it. Those people have been very, very, very
        wonderful people and the Lord will remember them too.
        They'll receive their reward . . .[42]

Story Four: BARRY MORGAN

For eight years from 1964 until 1972 Barry Morgan served as the
Ranch Manager at the New Mexico Boys Ranch. His connection to the
Ranch could well be viewed as one of God's mysterious ways.

Born on a farm near Portales in eastern New Mexico Morgan
graduated from Wayland Baptist College in Plainview, Texas in 1961.
He and his wife Martha then taught school for two years in the remote
Largo Canyon Area of northern New Mexico. As Morgan says, "We
were between the Apache and the Navajo Reservations. Equally
inaccessible from anywhere. It was a marvelous experience." Returning
to Portales for graduate school at Eastern New Mexico University the
Morgans took a job as houseparents at the Children's Home. By this time
Walker Hubbard was directing both the Children's Home and the Boys
Ranch. While working at the Children's Home one of the high school

students assigned to the Morgan house was a young man named Michael Kull, now President of the New Mexico Boys Ranch.

Morgan: Walker Hubbard was the encouragement for us to go to the Boys Ranch. When he asked me about going there I told him that I thought that I'd be ready in about ten years. He said, "Well, which do you think would be best? Go there and get the experience or wait ten years and then go get the experience?" And I had to agree. Another couple from Portales, Jerry and Iris Johnson, went with us.

Author: Were you in charge of everything?

Morgan: Yes, sir. There were about forty boys and we were quite idealistic when we moved in. We thought that by our going there and working hard all the kids would fall in and follow suit. It turned out to be more complicated than that. In the first week about a third of the kids ran away. Actually, the first day most of them didn't come home from school. They just got on trains, in buses, or hitchhiked and just left. We drove around day and night, as soon as the police picked them up we'd go and get them. The next week more left. That went on for six weeks. We were exhausted from just going day and night, just chasing runaways and not getting much else done. I called a meeting and said, if you leave you're on your own. I've driven my last mile because from now on my time is going to be spent making this a good place for those who want to stay. That helped some, but the first year was pretty hellacious.

          . . . The big problem was there was no money. In 1964 we could have sold everything, land, buildings, etc. and there would have remained $150,000 indebtedness that couldn't be paid.

          . . . There was a struggle with the school and the community during the first week I was there. The president of the bank in Belen came out to visit and said, "This community

could do very well without the Boys Ranch. But this Boys
Ranch cannot survive without the community and its help.
I want to make sure you understand that and if you turn
out to be like some of your predecessors we don't want you."
I was offended of course.

Author: He meant that the bills weren't getting paid?

Morgan: Bills weren't getting paid, the kids were causing trouble in
school, they were running away, there was poor community
relations. I took his word to Walker Hubbard and we realized
that community relations were an important part of the job.
I joined the Rotary and met with school principals and teachers to assure them that we would work with them in every
way. If a kid was incorrigible we would take him out of
school and just leave him at the Ranch until we had him cor-
rigible. It took a couple of years and then things began to
settle down. After a couple of years we began to get out of
debt and pay our bills on time and that helped immensely.

. . . During that first six weeks I had a challenge from a
group of the older boys. They challenged me with, "Well,
what are you going to do about it?" Saying to me, "You
might take one of us, but you can't take all of us and we're
going to whip your butt." I said, "I think you better think
this over, because I'm here to stay and I'm going to run
things and I won't be the one to leave. I'm going to give
you five minutes to think this over." I walked out and came
back in five minutes and everybody was making their beds
and that was the last of it.

Author: Did you ever have to go to jail and bail them out?

Morgan: Yeah, of course, many times. For everything. One boy kept
hot wiring cars. His dad came and took him home. Then he
was arrested and sent to Springer. I went to see him, but
they wouldn't release him. He tried to escape and they put
him in solitary confinement. He called me from Albu-

querque to tell me he had run away and I asked him to come see me, but he didn't. Then he was picked up for armed robbery and sent to the pen by the time he was eighteen.

Author: Care to relate any other stories?

Morgan: Let me tell you about the most awesome experience we had in the whole eight years we were there. Larry came to us through the Juvenile Court System. He was very fast and made the football team, scoring nearly all the touchdowns that Belen High School made. He just took the ball and ran away and no one could catch him. In a sense, Larry did more for our community relations than anything we could have done because he became very popular through his prowess on the football field.

. . . We required the kids to attend church once a week and a lady at church took a special interest in Larry. She wanted to see him become a believer and join the Baptist church. On this particular Sunday she came down out of the choir loft, put her arms around him and asked him to walk the aisle and give his heart to Jesus. He refused and kind of made a joke of it. He was a big hero to the other kids at the Ranch and the whole community at this time. That afternoon he and a couple of boys went somewhere and had a couple of beers. When he came back the kids heard him joking about his experience that morning in church. "Well, I'll see you in Hell," was his comment. The next day he had a tonsillectomy scheduled and while there he had a cardiac arrest and died. The whole community was devastated. We had his memorial service in the gymnasium and it was full. Quite a number of kids adopted a close relationship with the Lord after that. I was months getting over that. It was a tragedy that impacted on all of us more than any other event.

. . . By 1972 my wife and I were totally burned out. It was

just too intense. I tried to do everything myself. Maybe I
helped to build a bridge to the community . . .[43]

Story Five: DOROTHY HUBBARD

Dorothy Dana Davison Hubbard the devoted life-long wife and
coworker of Walker Hubbard was born on July 18, 1905. Zinicide (named
for what was discovered on her grandfather's land), Missouri, near
Joplin, is now a ghost town but in those days, the old pioneer family of
the Davisons' basically had their own town. Dorothy says, "There were
seven children and as each married Grandfather (George Davison) gave
each something to make a living on. One had the grocery store, one
had the meat market, one ran the post office, and my father was on
the old family farm. We were the third generation born on that farm."

When she was eleven years old Dorothy's family moved first to
Kansas and then into Oklahoma. She graduated from Wakita High
School in 1921 at the age of fifteen. Because her parents thought that she
was too young to go away to college they all moved to Winfield, Kansas
where she attended Southwestern (today Southwestern State
University). After two years (typical Normal School training in those
days) she started teaching in the public schools. "My first teaching job
was in Northeastern Colorado, and that was like going to Europe now,
you know. When I left home my parents were weeping because I was
going so far away.

Author: Do you remember your first salary?

Hubbard: Yes, I do. Ninety-five dollars a month. We were pleased
               with that salary because it was getting close to the De-
               pression times and many were out of work.

Author: How did you meet your husband?

Hubbard: Well when my parents moved back to Joplin, I came back.
               I met my husband in Picher, Oklahoma (They were both
               teachers). He was a junior high coach and taught history

and geography. Then he coached basketball, baseball, and later football. But also he was selected to be principal and then superintendent.

Author: **Was his family from Oklahoma?**

Hubbard: They were Cherokee Indian. He was only a sixteenth but actually I thought he was full blood, the way he acted (she means quiet). His family made the Trail of Tears from North Carolina and his father was born in Indiana on the Trail. They settled near Carthage, Missouri. His uncles made the land run in Oklahoma—the sooners.

. . . His father was the manager of a big department store in Aftar. He (Hubbard) went to school at OBU (Oklahoma Baptist University) and was teaching at Picher when we met.

Author: **When did you get married?**

Hubbard: May 1, 1926 . . . we were going to be married in June but the preacher we wanted to use was moving from Aftar. We made up our minds and went to his house early on a Saturday morning. Their whole house was full of packing boxes so the preacher got one for his pedestal, put his material on it and his wife played "Here Comes the Bride" on her violin. In the process in came his father chuckling, he said, "I have flowers for the bride," and he handed me a bunch of fresh green onions.

Author: **What a sense of humor!**

Hubbard: Oh, all of them, they were Quaker. They laughed with their eyes, you know, they didn't make any noise. We had the wedding dinner in their house and I bowed my head but there was no sound. I kept my head bowed a little longer than I thought I ought to, and when I looked up every-body was eating. They were Quaker and each had said his own thank you and had gone ahead with their meal.

. . . We went to the Ozark for our honeymoon because we're Ozark into the heart. Then on to Pittsburgh (State University in Kansas) for Summer school.

. . . Picher didn't employ married women so we went to Seneca, New Mexico near Clayton. Hubbard was the principal (and she had 1st grade). After one year we moved to Boise City, Oklahoma and were there ten years . . . The famous Sandstorms were so bad that I could hardly talk. My children would come in the morning with their hair normal color and by night it would be grey. We knew we had to change.

Author: Is that how you got to New Mexico?

Hubbard: We had both wanted to be college teachers and had planned on going to Colombia University the next summer. Well, we had a letter from The Baptist Board in New Mexico about a Children's Home in Portales. We didn't even know there was a Portales.

At this point Mrs. Hubbard related to the author how they rejected the first two letters, then with the third letter they agreed to go take a look at the Children's Home. That was in 1936 at the height of the Depression and Mrs. Hubbard was really depressed. Four hundred dollar bread bill, etc. Fifty children and the hot water had to be heated on stoves. The Hubbards told the Board if they would put in hot water they would come for a year. They stayed almost thirty-five.

The story of the Hubbards and The Baptist Children's Home is a separate story which needs to be told in another book. Hopefully someone reading this will do so in the future.

Author: So tell me how Walker got involved with the Boys Ranch.

Hubbard: It was through Dr. Harry Stagg the Executive Secretary of

the Baptist work in New Mexico. Carl Brogan of Albuquerque told Dr. Stagg that the Ranch was broke and said,
"We're losing Boys Ranch." They offered to give the Boys
Ranch to the Baptists if Mr. Hubbard would take it. They
called us to Albuquerque to discuss it. I was sitting in the
lobby of the hotel when Carl Brogan came out and said,
"You know we just offered a man double his salary if he
would take the Boys Ranch and he told us, "No, I'm not
even considering it. I belong to the Children's Home. That
Board sets my salary. If I take this, you pay half of it. And
that'll take half of the load off the Children's home and
half off of you and the salary will be set by my Children's Home Board . . ." Walker was sort of on loan. When
he agreed to take charge of Boys Ranch, he also kept the
job at Portales and drove back and forth in his own car,
two hundred and thirty-nine miles.

. . . He'd get up at four o'clock in the morning and drive
down here and get here in time for breakfast. Then he'd
take care of business here, go over to the Ranch and do
the things that needed to be done. Go to Albuquerque and
take care of his Baptist Children's Home business because
they had the treasury there, which we insisted on, and
then drive home that night. He'd usually get home at one,
two o'clock in the morning. He did that to save hotel bills.
He came here (to Belen) one day a week. The Boys Ranch
had a resident manager.

Author: How many years did Mr. Hubbard drive back and forth
           like that?

Hubbard: Well he resigned in 1972. You're supposed to retire at 65
           but they asked him to stay on and he was 69. He retired
           from the Children's Home July 1st of 1971. Mike told me
           when he (Walker) came to the Ranch they had their busi-
           ness meeting and Walker projected things that were start-
           ed and how to carry on. When he got through he said,
           "Gentlemen, I'm offering my resignation." He walked out

the door. He never accepted a word of thanks, he never gave them an opportunity to express themselves. He just got in the car and came home.

Author: So he just walked away?

Hubbard: He just walked away! Barry Morgan (Ranch Manager) called me that night and he said, "He didn't even give us a chance to thank him! I said, "Barry, he's not made that way. He's a reserved man and he controls his emotions." That was a difficult decision for him but he reached the point where he felt like "I've done my work, I've sung my song."

Walker Hubbard died in 1977 at the age of seventy-five.[44]

NOTES

1. Minutes Board of Directors July 26, 1954.
2. Ibid.
3. Baptist New Mexican, N.M.B.R. Files, September 9, 1954.
4. Annual Meeting of Board of Directors January 31, 1955.
5. Ibid.
6. Ibid.
7. Baptist New Mexico news clipping undated N.M.B.R. Files.
8. Files N.M.B.R. undated.
9. Minutes New Mexico Boys Ranch January (no day), 1956.
10. Ibid.
11. Minutes Annual Meeting N.M.B.R. January 27, 1957.
12. Ibid.
13. January 4, 1958 Minutes.
14. Ibid and Executive Board Meeting April 10, 1957.
15. Files N.M.B.R.
16. Memorandum dated January 4, 1958 N.M.B.R. Files.
17. Ibid.
18. Ibid.
19. Progress Report January 1958 to January 1959 N.M.B.R. Files.
20. Annual Minutes January 26, 1959.
21. Ibid.

22. Letter dated June 11, 1959 N.M.B.R. Files.
23. Papers dated December 31, 1959 N.M.B.R. Files.
24. Annual Minutes January 25, 1960.
25. Ibid.
26. Progress Report of 1960 N.M.B.R.
27. Summer Minutes July 14, 1961.
28. N.M.B.R. Files.
29. Annual Minutes January 29, 1962.
30. N.M.B.R. Files Assumed to be October 1965.
31. Annual Minutes January 31, 1966.
32. Annual Minutes January 28, 1967.
33. Report of Boys' Achievements for 1967 N.M.B.R.
34. New Mexico Boys Ranch Report January 1, 1968.
35. Letter from Walker Hubbard October 2, 1968 N.M.B.R.
36. N.M.B.R. Files.
37. Letter from Walker Hubbard June 22, 1971 N.M.B.R.
38. Undated, unsigned letter N.M.B.R. Files late 1960s.
39. Quoted in *Harry P. Stagg: Christian Statesman* (Broadman Press, Nashville, Tenn., 1976) p. 8.
40. Interview with Harry P. Stagg, June 27, 1991 Albuquerque, New Mexico.
41. Interview with Carter Waid, June 26, 1991, Belen, New Mexico.
42. Interview with Wayne Britton, May 20, 1992, Fort Worth, Texas.
43. Interview with Barry Morgan, May 20, 1992, Fort Worth, Texas.
44. Interview with Dorothy Hubbard, June 24, 1991, Belen, New Mexico.

Chapter Five
TIMES CHANGE AND
PEOPLE CHANGE

The year 1970 was marked by violence across America as college students continued to protest the war in Vietnam. At Kent State in Ohio National Guardsmen opened fire killing four students and wounding nine. America was uneasy and the New York Stock Market hit an eight year low with the Dow-Jones Industrial Average dropping to 631.

In New Mexico at the Boys Ranch major changes in personnel were about to happen. Meanwhile, the first order of business of the Annual Meeting of the Board of Directors was the replacement of Carl Brogan who had just died. Faithful steward Carter Waid was elected and tribute was also paid to the deceased Dub Evans and J.W. Wilfreth. The old guard was passing. In addition to Waid, who served as secretary again, Holm Bursum was again elected president. Other officers that year were J.B. Tidwell, Lucille Green, and Andy Sutter.[1]

When the meeting got to Ranch Manager Morgan's report he noted the livestock as: 133 head of cattle, 25 horses, 2 mules, 5 sows and 2 boars, 50 chickens, 10 sheep, and 1 registered goat. Morgan read a letter to the gathering from a Belen school teacher complimenting them, (the boys) on their behavior. Next, one of the boys (Richard Bradford) recited his award winning oration called "Freedom Challenge." This stirring piece of original work had won him the Voice of Democracy Award at Belen High School that year.

All assembled at the annual meeting were truly delighted when it was announced that Dr. and Mrs. (Jackie) Spencer of Carrizozo wished to donate $50,000 toward the cost of a new cottage for 16 boys. This new building was named the Bancroft Cottage because the money came from the Bancroft Foundation. (Mrs. Spencer's former husband was Dr. Bancroft.) With the help of another $40,000 from the Max C. Fleischmann Foundation of Reno, Nevada, and donations from the New Mexico Cowbelles, the new dining room became a reality. When dedicated it bore the name of Dub Evans, a former Board Member and well-known rancher from Magdalena.

In January 1971 Barry Morgan presented the Board with the results of a Six Year Progress Report. This report was the result of work done by former houseparents, Mr. & Mrs. Jerry Johnson, as part of their college work at Eastern New Mexico University. While this actual report is no longer available for examination we do have the words of Morgan to the effect that, "If success is considered as not getting into trouble with law enforcement officers, then the Ranch has been over 80 percent successful in the past six years."[2]

Significant for the future was the fact that at this January meeting the charter and bylaws were revised and approved. These changes called for a twenty-one member board with each member serving a three year term. Seven new members would be elected each year. At this meeting new names appearing on the Board for the first time included George Rutherford and Wilfred Clarke of Albuquerque. Also approved at this meeting was the official relocation of the Ranch office to Belen.

It is intriguing to examine the list of the various stock shares that had been given to the Ranch through wills and estates. By 1971 the two largest gifts were 1,824 shares of the Putnam Growth Fund and 1,000 shares of Ultra Marble, Inc. The same financial report listed $50,000 in Certificates of Deposit at the Citizens Bank in Clovis and $2,132.27 in a savings account at the same bank.[3]

At the August 30, 1971 meeting Ranch Manager Morgan urged the Board to relocate Mike Kull, the Director of Development, to Belen by leasing a residential property. This was approved with the requirement that, "The Director of Development shall be required to live in a home owned or leased by the New Mexico Boys Ranch in order to service the in-town boys."[4]

Statistics relating to the boys were released at the August meeting. The figures indicate that for the year of 1970 some seventy boys had been cared for at the Ranch. Of this number sixteen had been released to relatives and one joined the Armed Service. Of the fifty boys living at the Ranch on January 1, 1971 twenty-seven were from Bernalillo County. A total of twelve different counties were represented by the various boys.

On March 30, 1972 by the action of the Board of Directors the first retirement program for employees of the Ranch was established. In layman's terms this was a life insurance based retirement endowment plan between the Ranch, as a company, and the New York Life Insurance Company. The first group of employees eligible for this new plan were Barry Morgan, Mike and Nikki Kull, and Gerry Lowrance. New board members attending their first meeting that day were Jack Ratliff and Albert Michell.[5]

It is interesting to note that on August 24, 1972 Barry and Martha Morgan, who had been at the Ranch eight years, resigned and were replaced immediately by Michael H. Kull, the Director of Development. While not one word is mentioned in the official minutes of this meeting, sometime earlier that summer Walker Hubbard had submitted his resignation. Interviews with Mrs. Hubbard indicate that Hubbard retired from the Children's Home in Portales in 1971 and the next summer (1972) from the Boys Ranch. Several witnesses indicated that at the conclusion of the business meeting he offered his resignation and walked out the door. (The author believes that a set of minutes is missing from the records for this time period. Mike Kull remembers Hubbard resigning prior to the August 24th meeting date.) Perhaps someday there will be an appropriate statue of this incredible, dignified man placed on the campus at the Boys Ranch. Walker Hubbard passed on to his reward on September 24, 1977.

During that same summer of change at the Ranch there occurred a wonderful human interest story about one of the boys. Jimmy was a sixth-grade student who suffered from diabetes. It seems that young Jimmy wrote to the Army recruiter at Albuquerque expressing his desire to serve in the Army. Knowing that Jimmy would never be accepted into any branch of the service because of his illness, the recruiter arranged for Major General Woodbury to commission him an honorary corporal in the U.S. Army. Two years later this gutsy honor-roll student was selected to study in Europe for the summer. Thanks to help from several board members and the New Mexico Hairdressers Association this young boy had the trip of a lifetime.

In a rather interesting political move (and in agreement with the IRS) Ranch attorney Charles N. Glass, a member of the Board, called the

January 29, 1973 annual meeting to order and was then elected chairman. He announced that the first order of business was to determine the credentials of all board members present. Once this occurred new elections were held for all officers and two board positions. Elected unanimously were the following:

President   - B.G. Barnes
Vice-President   - J.B. Tidwell
Secretary   - Arno Romero
Treasurer   - Barbara Nicholson
Superintendent   - Michael Kull
Board members included:
Ted Bonnell, Jack Ratliff, W.A. Sutter, and J.A. May.[6]

What seems to have happened in the early 1970s was that some board members continued to serve after their term expired (under the new system), while others became less interested and did not participate on a regular basis. Obviously, it succeeded for the same set of officers were reelected each year for the next several years.

More serious was the financial report of the same meeting. Reflecting the sharp turn downward of the national stock market the Ranch sustained approximately a $4,000 loss in share decreases. Board member Ratliff, who made this report, recommended staying with the Mutual Fund until the loss could be recovered then switching into other programs. This action was carried out over a number of years, but a loss was recorded.[7]

Superintendent Kull outlined an ambitious Farm Development Program to the Board on July 20, 1973. It was estimated that if implemented the plan would take some seven years to complete. Among other things this plan was to help train boys in the scientific development and management of a ranch. Some 800 acres were to be used to expand the cattle herd by about four times. A new Butler Building was to be built for use of the livestock and the old dining room would be used to house new farm equipment. Financially this program, which was approved, was to be funded by the sale of the Mutual Funds, surplus funds from several estates, and leftover funds from the construction of the dining room. The intended goal was to reduce the dependency on public aid by increasing the Ranch income. It was also hoped that this would allow an increase in the number of boys cared for and the establishment of satellite care centers.[8]

At the annual meeting of the Board of Directors held on January 28, 1974 all officers from the previous year were unanimously reelected. At the same time Jess May and Albert Mitchell were reelected to a full three year term on the Board. Out of the minutes of this meeting comes mention that for the first time ever the Ranch was able to provide for an extended vacation for some of the boys. One dormitory visited Six Flags Over Texas (near Dallas) and one dormitory traveled by van all the way to Disneyland in California.[9]

An analysis of the proposed 1974 budget (expected to be $190,829.94) revealed that in 1973 the Ranch had actually spent fifteen percent less than the budgeted amount ($174,500 out of $189,218). At the same time there were more boys handled in 1973 than in 1972. It is also interesting to note that the old La Jolla School Buildings were offered to the Ranch. While the price was right, the buildings (all 13 of them) were old and extensive maintenance would have been required. The offer was rejected.[10]

Three items of future interest appear in these same January, 1974 documents. One, the first mention of a new address appears—New Mexico Boys Ranch, Boys Ranch, New Mexico. Two, Mrs. Alice King, the Governor's wife, agreed to discuss the post office issue with state officials. Three, Ted Bonnell of Bank Security, Inc. offered a free lunch so that the boys, staff and directors could meet the famous Dr. Norman Vincent Peale while he was in Albuquerque.[11]

During 1973-74, and at Ted Bonnell's urging, B.S.I. (Bank Securities, Inc.) employees pledged at least ten dollars a year to the Boys Ranch. Their specific goal was to provide the funds for a new dormitory especially for the "little boys." They raised some $42,000 which was not the total cost of the building, but did enable the Ranch to start construction. At the same meeting Charles Gibson of the staff presented an insurance consolidation report. Simply stated Southwest Insurance Company was to cover the buildings, the retirement system stayed with New York Life and Blue Cross and Blue Shield was to provide the health care coverage. As Gibson says, "We may be the only Boys Ranch in the U.S. to have health coverage of this type for the boys."[12] Perhaps even more unique was the hand carved wooden sign which arrived from the inmates at the Santa Fe Prison. This sign, which now hangs in the gym reads, "New Mexico Boys Ranch: Where a Fellow Can Get a Fresh Start."[13]

For the third straight year all of the same officers were reelected on January 27, 1975 with B.G. Barnes again serving as President. When Superintendent Kull made his annual report he noted that the total cost of the B.S.I. Building (new dormitory) was $58,360 and the new gym would cost $66,670 After much discussion the Board voted to finish off both buildings using CDs and general funds while seeking new sources of income. Tommy Dils, owner of a Belen based construction company, was given a vote of appreciation for his building program supervision over the past several years.[14]

The downward price of beef in the U.S. market is reflected in Kull's Farm Report of 1975. He recommended that one-half of the herd be sold both to save feed bills and to help pay off the farm expansion program. The sale was estimated to be worth twelve thousand dollars. Once again, as he had done several times in the past, Al Mitchell offered to donate enough heifers to build up the herd in the future. Kull's report also indicated that there had been sixty-two boys cared for at the Ranch during the past year. There had been one hundred and thirty-one referrals from some twenty-four towns and twenty-one of these had been accepted.[15]

Two items that will be significant in the future first appeared in 1975. One is the first mention of a new property. At that time a portion of the Hart Ranch was up for sale by the trustees and the Boys Ranch merely asked that their interests be kept in mind by the owners. The other item concerns Mike Kull's suggestion to the Board that in the future the Ranch should seriously consider starting a Girls Ranch. Apparently several other groups were interested in the idea and Kull suggested that the Ranch lawyer (Charles Glass) be instructed to copyright the names "New Mexico Girls Ranch" and "Girls Ranch." While it would take a number of years for both of these projects to come to fruition, the seeds had been planted.[16]

Statistical reports for 1975 reveal, among other things, that the Ranch now had sixteen full-time employees; two hundred and thirty head of cattle; forty-seven horses and mules; a bank balance of $58,375.96; and was valued at $1,139,016.24. Once again Bernalillo County led the list of donors followed in order by Chaves, Santa Fe, Dona Ana, Eddy, Quay, Vallencia, and Lea.[17]

Farm manager Don Vestal reported in October that the Ranch had put up 500 tons of ensilage corn, 100 tons of alfalfa, and about 1,000 bales of oat hay and wheat grass. At the time of his report there were 150 acres of wheat grass, 17 acres of oats, 45 acres of corn, and 130 acres of winter wheat.[18]

During 1976 the U.S. celebrated its Bicentennial by marking the 200th anniversary of its Independence with numerous festivals and parades. In New York City, Operation Sail, a gathering of tall ships from around the world, was viewed by some six million persons. It is ironic that the very year that the nation was celebrating its Independence the Ranch was worried about theirs, for by 1976 governmental interference with the operation of the Ranch had become a major concern. At the January 26, 1976 meeting the Advisors requested the Directors to enter a formal resolution not to accept federal or state funds or controls wherever possible. Thus by a unanimous vote the following resolution was adopted:

> That the New Mexico Boys Ranch not accept federal or state funding and resist all attempts to interfere with or control the operation of the Ranch by federal or state agencies or individuals.[19]

Later that same year the Ranch turned down an offer by the state to pay for a portion of each boys meals not eaten in school. Time and time again the Ranch has made it a point to remain as private and independent as possible.

While various officers and board members are frequently mentioned in the annual reports and records that is not always the case with the "Advisors." One of the few existing lists is from the year 1976 and they are listed as follows:

> John Moore (Roswell), Clovis Evans (Artesia), Harry Latham (Deming), Buck Pruit (Deming), Mark Sloan (Alamogordo), Patricia and Ted Garoutte (Bluewater Lake), Ben Woodward (Las Cruces), Dorothy and Carl Trembly (Gallup), Lucille Green (Hobbs), Roland and Mary Pettitt (Los Alamos), Alice

King (Stanley), Earl and Rosalie Shelton (Santa Fe), and Carter Waid (Belen).[20]

On June 30, 1977 a two year building project was culminated with the dedication of the Mike Horn Memorial Gymnasium. Mr. & Mrs. Calvin Horn of Albuquerque gave the major portion of funds for the building in memory of their son who was killed in a plane accident in the Philippines. This 9,000 square foot building included a basketball court, boxing ring, wrestling mats, showers and lockers, and two classrooms for arts and crafts. Much free labor on this project was donated by several unions in Albuquerque.[21]

On the same June day, at the gym dedication, Superintendent Charles Gibson announced to the Board that Clyde Tyler of Albuquerque had committed himself to $27,000 toward a new office, library, and clinic building. Bank Securities Incorporated pledged another $15,000 toward the new project, and Mr. and Mrs. Clyde Jones of Albuquerque made a major donation. Numerous firms, organizations and individuals gave materials, furnishings and labor to complete this building. When dedicated on March 13, 1978 the new structure marked several "firsts" for the Ranch. For example, it was the first building to be solar heated, the first time the Ranch had a clinic, the first library of adequate size and shelving, and the first actually designated office.[22]

Throughout the 1970s the Boys Ranch was blessed with help from a large number of very famous people. For example, Larry Mahan, the six time All Around World Champion Cowboy, provided free radio spots for the Annual Boys Ranch Rodeos. Others included Don Perkins, former all-star halfback for the Dallas Cowboys and sportscaster for an Albuquerque radio and television station. Folk singer Burl Ives, country singers Charlie Pride, Roy Clark and Glen Campbell all cut special promotionals without any charge to the Ranch. To top it all off Ernest Borgnine, a well-known movie actor and television star, actually came down to the Boys Ranch (1978) and spent some time visiting the boys, and later also did a Public Service Announcement.

For years Bill Swanwick and Jan Arrington of Swanwick Advertising wrote all of the promotional spots and made all arrangements for each production. KOAT television usually taped the spots in their studios. The tapes were then duplicated by Jim Aubel of Station KOB and sent to seven television stations and forty radio stations in New Mexico and Texas.

As the decade of the seventies drew to a close Executive Director Michael H. Kull is quoted as saying, "I believe that 1979 will be remembered as an important year of decision at Boys Ranch, a turning point in our development."[23] The background behind this bold statement was the fact that each year saw an increasing number of referrals of troubled boys being made to the Ranch. Additionally, the leadership was keenly aware of the growing number of girls that needed help. It was obvious that while more and more girls desperately needed long-term help, the State of New Mexico had very few resources available.[24]

Thus it was that the Board of Directors and the Advisors decided to reach out boldly in both directions. Spearheaded by Alice King, New Mexico's First Lady and newly elected member of the Board, a special new Girls Ranch was to be built near Santa Fe. At the same time, the decision was made to build a satellite Boys Ranch on the Hart Ranch property south of Melrose, near Portales.[25]

By October 1979 with very little capital reserve in hand both projects started forward. For example, the fifth annual cattle drive focused on gathering together about 100 heifers to form a new herd at the Hart Ranch. The new decade seemed to be envisioned in Kull's words to the many Ranch supporters when he wrote:

> With your help and God's blessing there will be boys and girls who will find the home and love they need to grow up because of the sacrifice we are willing to make. It can be done if we all work together.[26]

Story One: THE BLEVINS FAMILY

Helenita, Otis, Iris, and Jim Blevins all worked for the Boys Ranch at one time or another between the years 1968 and 1974. How they arrived at the Boys Ranch and their experiences there are all part of the unique stories that have played a role in the history of the Ranch. What follows are excerpts from a lengthy interview with the Blevins in Clovis, New Mexico on June 16, 1991.

Otis (the father) was born in 1916 at Harrison, Arkansas. At a relatively young age he moved to Eureka, Kansas where he met Helenita at a local dance. In 1938 at the height of the Great Depression and four years after Helenita's high school graduation this young couple married. When Otis was asked by the author how he got from Kansas to New Mexico he replied, "My wife came out here on vacation and I was driving truck (in Kansas). When I heard they was hirin' men on the Santa Fe Railroad I just quit and caught a bus and came out here." That was in 1941. World War II had started and there was lots of railroad traffic going through the yards in Belen.

Helenita was the first of the family to go to work for the Boys Ranch. When asked how and why she was hired Helenita replied as follows: "Sid Riley and his wife were houseparents out there and Wanda (Riley) asked me to come out there and cook for them. I said, 'Well, I'll try it.' So I went out and started. I went out two days and worked and then I just started in. There was about fifty people to cook for."

Author: Did you both (Otis and Helenita) move from Belen out to the Ranch?

Helenita: Oh, yes. He (Otis) was still working on the railroad as a switchman. He came out in the evenings. And then on Saturdays he'd ride (horses) and work a little bit with the boys.

Author: Iris, how did you and Jim come to work for the Ranch?

Iris: Through my mother and father-in-law. They said there was an opening for houseparents with the younger boys. We were young. I was nineteen and he (Jim) was twenty-three. We had just gotten married and we really didn't have anything going for us. So we went to be houseparents for the younger boys.

Author: Who interviewed you or hired you?

Iris: Barry Morgan was the boss. It wasn't run as formally when we were there. It was like a home . . . it wasn't the business it is today. We had the smaller boys like six through twelve at the old Ranch house "up top." It was a mile from "down bottom." That was the terminology. All total there were three or four couples as houseparents. The house "up top" was adobe and each dorm room had three or four beds. Most of the other buildings were quonset huts.

Author: **Iris, as a house parent what kind of chores were these younger boys expected to do?**

Iris: They cleaned their part of the dorm, mopped and waxed the floors, cleaned the toilets and sinks. They collected the laundry and took it "down bottom" to Mella (Torres) and then brought it back up. They fed the animals.

Author: **Did you ever have to punish them?**

Iris: We whipped some of ours. We just treated them like they were our own children.

Author: **Where did these boys go to school?**

Iris: In Belen. My husband was the bus driver and he would bring the bus home, park it at the Boys Ranch, and then take all the boys to town the next day. It was a regular bus route. He was paid by both the Ranch and the school district. During the day he worked at the school bus barn in town.

Author: **Did you take the boys to church?**

Iris: Most of us went to the Baptist Church in Belen. Some of the boys went to the little Catholic Church outside of Belen. When some of the boys got older and could drive they went there. They had their choice.

Author: **Were drugs and alcohol a problem in those days?**

Iris: Alcohol, yes. Once some of the older boys broke into the kitchen and stole the vanilla for the alcohol in it. They used to sniff gasoline. We had three or four boys do that. We had to watch them pretty close. The older ones would try to bring beer and sometimes marijuana from school and try to hide it in their toilet tank. Not much drugs in those days.

Author: **Helenita, what was it like to cook for fifty people?**

Helenita: Well, I got most everything I wanted to cook with. We'd have lots of bacon and eggs and toast and biscuits for breakfast. Lots of macaroni and cheese. Holidays we'd have the full turkey dinner and pumpkin pie and pecan pie. One boy learned to cook and the last I knew he was cooking at the country club in Belen. At least three boys went into some kind of food preparation service. When I started we were in that old quonset hut. On Saturdays we would get down on our hands and knees and scrub that cement floor. Of course, it didn't last long (stay clean), but we did it.

Author: **What were houseparents paid in the late '60s?**

Iris: Probably like two hundred and fifty dollars per month, plus food and housing. There were no fringe benefits nor retirement. We paid our own medical, telephone calls, and personal gas. We were on six days a week with Monday off and one weekend off a month. It was a very emotional job because you got involved in their hearts, you know? You couldn't just work there and not get involved in their lives and what was going on.

When asked by the author to talk about special incidents that they remembered or special boys the Blevins replied as follows:

Helenita: Well, Henry and Roy were really good kids. Otis piped in and said, "They was the best." From what I understand their mother took them to the Ranch and said that she would be back in six weeks. They were maybe nine or ten years old. She came back once—for their graduation

Iris: We had two boys named Joey and John. The story goes that their mother told them to get dressed one night. "Get your baths; get your pajamas; get clean clothes." She then took them to the police department and turned them in as incorrigibles. They were probably eight or nine at the time they came to the Ranch.

. . . then there was Clay. He was nine when he came to us. He had walked into a U.S. Post Office, walked behind the counter, and stole some money. He didn't intentionally rob the U.S. Post Office, but that's how he ended up there (at the Ranch).

Otis: Barry Morgan, Joe Roberson and I would take about sixteen boys up to the Pecos Wilderness and stay for three to five nights. We taught the boys how to cook and how to find their way around in the mountains. Sometimes the snow was still up to the knees on the horses. They learned a lot by going on those trips.

Iris: We would all go to the State Fair and they'd let us in free. We took them in the bus. And if we went to the drive-in at night we'd park the bus sideways and take up several speakers and just put them in the bus. They (the theater) didn't charge at all. Around Belen they knew you were from the Boys Ranch. One guy gave all the boys free haircuts. Sometimes he or others would come out to the Ranch to give the haircuts. The doctors donated their time and whatever. The local business people were very supportive of the Ranch when we were there.

Iris: There really is a funny story. We took one boy in for a tonsillectomy. While on the operating table the doctor noticed that his stomach was red and protruding. That was a full bladder! So he checked him out further and found that he needed to be circumcised. He was twelve or thirteen and had some infection due to non-circumcision. So they circumcised him at the same time they did the tonsillectomy. Well, when he came out from underneath the sedative he was asking Jim, my husband, "Pop, if I had my tonsils taken out, why does it hurt down there?"[27]

Story Two: BILLIE HOLDER

Mr. Billie Holder was born in eastern Oklahoma in 1914 just a few short years after statehood. His family reaches back into the early Indian Territory days where his grandfather had served as a federal marshall. Holder's mother was a full-blooded Indian. In due time he graduated from Salasome, Oklahoma High School. Unlike the many other Oklahomans who came to New Mexico, it wasn't the Dust Bowl but rather the climate brought Holder west. As a life-long sufferer of asthma Holder found that the combination of elevation, dry climate and low humidity helped him to breathe better. Indeed, at age 87 when interviewed, Holder seemed like an advertisement for the local Chamber of Commerce.

By purchasing the weekly newspaper in Alamogordo Holder, in effect, became a New Mexican businessman. Through the years his business prospered and he found himself serving a variety of civic and church positions. He has served as the District Governor of the Rotary Clubs, Chairman of the State Board of Economic Development, and was a member of the Board of Directors of the Boys Ranch.

When Holder was asked by this author how he first got involved with the Boys Ranch he replied as follows:

Holder: I was interested in helping boys and have been interested in scouting all my life. (The plaques on his office walls attest to this fact.) I also got acquainted with the Baptist Orphans home in Portales and with Walker Hubbard (Holder is a life-long Baptist). (With a twinkle in his eye Holder said), There's no orphans anymore, you know? So it's become a children's home, not an orphan's home. The point is they

(Boys Ranch) were an independent group totally free from any government monies of any kind and they wanted to stay that way.

Author: **Did you know that Walker Hubbard was also from Oklahoma and of Indian ancestry?**

Holder: I didn't really know that. Anyhow, I got well acquainted with him, just simply because of my interest in youth at the time. What they wanted at the Boys Ranch was to have a Board because of the legal setup, the incorporation, and that sort of thing. And yet they didn't want anybody who would come in and interfere with the operation of the Ranch or the home (Children's Home) either for that matter. They wanted somebody who would be on the Board, almost a "yes-man" for the Board members, but would let them run it. It didn't bother me a whole lot. Main thing is I used it for the placement of incorrigible kids around town here (Alamogordo), as a place to put them and almost as a threat, you know? I fit the bill of what they wanted and so I served. And that was my attitude! They'd call me on the phone every once in a while and I went over there a time or two for annual meetings and things of that nature

Author: **When you went on the Board (early '70s) do you have any recollection as to what kind of financial shape it was in?**

Holder: Oh . . . begging. They were always begging. They always had a need for finances. I made speeches, mostly to Rotary, service groups, and community people, all over the State of New Mexico . . . bragging about the fact that we don't take any government money of any kind.

Author: **You said that you didn't generate much financial support or particular interest here in Alamogordo. Why?**

Holder: No particular (reason) . . . most people don't know about

the needs of kids. When they get in trouble...they don't
know anything about it, unless they go to jail or something
like that. If someone is really raising Cain about it, why
they might become interested, that's largely it. They just
don't know about it. I think people, in general, will support
what they like, when they know about it and what they are
acquainted with, financially. If they don't know about it,
they're not going to give no matter who you are or where
you come from.

Author: Did you personally get involved with some of the boys
          that went to the Ranch?

Holder: Yes, three or four that were troublemakers in high school.
          I'd get calls at Midnight, you know? Mostly they were not
          the criminal sorts. They were juvenile delinquents, more
          than anything else.

Author: As you saw it, was it an alternative for reform school?

Holder: It was an alternative for the courts. I've gone to the courts
          here many times and he (the judge) would say, "Can you
          take this boy?" Then I'd have to call over (to the Ranch)
          and find out if we had room for him. Then the judge would
          explain to him (the boy) that, "It is a private Ranch and you
          will have to work as a ranch hand. It's gonna be tough,
          you're gonna sweat . . . Any time that you don't want that
          I can send you to Springer. It's a prison, (Springer that is),
          it's not a Ranch."

Author: Did you ever write any newspaper stories about the
          Ranch?

Holder: Yes, I did and I have a daughter and son-in-law who were
          houseparents there for a year. Today I am in partnership
          with both the Boys and the Girls Ranch (meaning that
          Holder sends a monthly donation for each).[28]

Story Three: BILLY G. BARNES

Billy G. Barnes represents one of those Albuquerque businessmen who got interested in the Boys Ranch. Starting out by playing Santa Claus, Barnes ended up by serving on the Board of Directors, five years of which he served as president.

Born in Monroe, Oklahoma in 1930 Barnes was quite literally part of the Dust Bowl migration to California when he was seven years old.

Author: **From your point of view was The Grapes of Wrath story a true perspective?**

Barnes: From my perspective it was totally real. We camped on the desert, arrived in California with ten cents in our pocket. I was seven years old, and a very, very true part of the movie "Grapes of Wrath." I sat there and watched it and saw myself during the whole trip.

Author: **Do you remember Oklahoma? Was your dad a farmer?**

Barnes: I was raised on the eastern side of Oklahoma. My father was a carpenter by trade and, of course, when the other people left Oklahoma it became a very distressed state and we had to go. Fortunately, he got a job shortly after we got there and our family did very well after that. In the late 1950s we moved back to Oklahoma as my dad wanted a business for himself. I spent two years with the 24th Army Division in Korea and then worked for Color Tile in Denver. My family moved to Albuquerque in 1961 to build, manage and open a store here. I went into business and sold out in 1979. Since then I've been in about five businesses. It's very hard to retire.

Author: **How did you get involved with the New Mexico Boys Ranch?**

Barnes: About 1963 or '64 my family heard of the Boys Ranch and the work they were doing. A particular thing we liked about it was the fact that it was not federally or state funded. We were young and coming up in the business world. We wanted a charity that we could latch onto that we knew our monies that we were giving them were being put to a good use. The New Mexico Boys Ranch was one of those areas we looked at through acquaintances we met. We met Superintendent Barry Morgan and his wife and we liked them and what they were doing. At that time they were in desperate straights. We decided to do what we could to help them.

Author: Was it through your contributions that you got named to the Board of Directors?

Barnes: I don't believe so. Our entire family did personal work, more than actual money. The Ranch you see today is like night and day from what we had then. At that point we had an old army quonset hut as a dining hall. When it snowed it came in under the building about a foot-and-a half into the building itself. The food was donated. We gathered toys and fixed them. We gathered clothes and mended them. At that time I believe there was a total of four buildings on the entire twenty-two hundred acres. Barry Morgan was an individual who thought more of other people than he did of himself, and they were struggling. Their entire budget for the whole year was seventy-nine to eighty thousand dollars and they were eighty thousand dollars in debt.

... At that time I weighed about three hundred and seventy-five pounds and didn't have to use a pillow. I guess I played Santa Claus for about five or six years in a row down there. We would cajole our friends and get gifts. The New Mexico Cowbelles donated clothing and it was a hand-to-mouth existence.

Author: By 1974-75 there seemed to be a whole new Board. Whose idea was it to have an active Board instead of a rather passive Board?

Barnes: This came from the Superintendent, Barry Morgan, who was a very close friend of mine at that time. We went hunting with the boys, did personal work out in the field and out in the mountains, which is where you can really work with them. We got to talking about the fact that the Ranch was going nowhere. We needed a working Board which we didn't have.

We still had old buildings, we were struggling, still in debt, no perks for the employees. Barry needed a new Board to get the Ranch started right. We came up with a strategy, if you want to call it that. I obtained proxies from the people who had the voting power and attended the Annual Meeting in 1974. I was not a member of the Board at that time, but I had these proxies, enough to override any "nay" vote that the Board might come up with during this meeting. Barry asked the existing Board to resign, doing it as diplomatically as he could, indicating that he needed people to work with the Ranch. The existing Board had their own businesses to run. They had been a member of the Board for many, many years. Generally, everybody went along (with the IRS recommendation) so they could get the meeting over and get home.

Author: These men were from the days when Walker Hubbard kind of ran everything?

Barnes: Right, right. Fortunately, the Board agreed, not happily, I think, but they agreed to resign. Some of them felt bad about it. Others actually agreed with us and the new Board was appointed at that time.

Author: Who were some of the new men that expressed an interest in getting more involved and who stayed on?

Barnes: Oh, people like Bob Davis, Jack Ratliff, Ted Bonnell, people like that who were working at the Ranch at the time but didn't have the decision-making process that was necessary.

[Author's note: Some of the members of the new Board, like J.B. Tidwell from Hobbs, and Andy Sutter from Clovis, had served for years and continued to serve.

Barnes: The ones on the Board that had been working, they were kept and they did a very credible and very good job. I was appointed to the Board of Directors and a few years later was appointed Chairman of the Board (a post he held for five years).

Author: Mr. Barnes, were you responsible for hiring Mike Kull?

Barnes: To a degree. I did not initiate it, but I certainly placed my vote for him and he's been the best we've ever had, outside of Barry Morgan. Now Barry had the desire and the hands and the so-called logic to run the Ranch, but he lacked the administrative bookkeeping stuff that Mike has. Mike Kull is a combination of two or three things that we had three people doing. Mike Kull does all of them. One of the things he did that started the Ranch off was (to) hire Charlie Gibson, who is very administrative oriented from the standpoint of fund raising. He worked many and long hours getting wills and trusts set up. During that period of time we jumped up and down if we got two a year. Now, of course, we have many, many of them coming in all the time.

Author: What's the best experience that you've personally had with the Ranch?

Barnes: After working a few years down there, the Santa Claus bit, going out on camping trips with the boys and fishing trips, it got to where when I came down to the Ranch the little fellas would run up and grab me around the leg and look up at me and say, "It's Santa Claus" and "It's Uncle Bill." Having seen the boy when he first came to the Ranch and then seeing him, you know, six months or a year later. . . a happy individual that you know is going to go out and mean something to other people in his own life.

. . . Probably the crowning good thing that happened to me down there was that one year, without me knowing it, the boys worked with Barry Morgan and took an old 25-06 rifle and made me a handmade laminated stock. They reglued the rifle. My mother-in-law sent the scope down and those boys put me together a beautiful, beautiful handmade rifle. After I played Santa Claus that particular year they brought me in and gave me that surprise gift of that rifle. That's probably the best thing that ever happened to me and I still have the rifle.[29]

Story Four: TED BONNELL

Born in Alamogordo, New Mexico on May 20, 1928 Ted Bonnell grew up on ranches in the mountains near Cloudcroft. After attending public school for eleven years in Tularosa, Bonnell transferred to the New Mexico Military Institute. Later at New Mexico A&M (now New Mexico State University) he majored in Animal Husbandry. Ted Bonnell was an extremely active member of the Board of Directors during the 1970s and served several terms as president of that body.

Author: Did you (as a New Mexican businessman) know Al Buck the founder of the Boys Ranch?

Bonnell: I have met Al Buck and Mr. Hubbard. Holm Bursum and I were always great friends and I think he called on me a couple of times to assist in some endeavors for the Ranch. Holm was President of the Board for a number of years. He and some of the other fellas raised the money to keep that thing (the Ranch) going during the hard tough times.

... I was really involved after Mike Kull got there. I know that on a number of occasions, Mike would call me in Alamogordo and say, "Ted, we have to have five hundred dollars to eat the rest of the month." You felt the pressure and you had the responsibility. You either raised the five hundred or you sent it because those boys had to eat. I want to say that if I've ever known real Christians in my life it's Mike Kull and Charles Gibson and their wives. Those fellas have given their lives, their energy, their inspiration for the boys and so unselfishly. It was always an inspiration to me to do more. I've known some great Christians, but I've never known any stronger than those people.

Author: Wow, what a testimony!

Bonnell: Also, the people they've been able to get as houseparents to help them in the endeavor and even the Board members. It's really been an inspiration just to work with those people and be involved. I've been very fortunate. I did the first bank holding company in New Mexico and when I sold control in 1980 we had over five hundred employees. It was through all of these people that I was really able to help. And I have a real fine feeling in my tummy for what all of us in B.S.I. (Bank Securities, Inc.) were able to do for the Ranch. At least once a year we would hold one of the board meetings at the Ranch, say in conjunction with the Albuquerque Bank Board. One man was so impressed with the caliber of people that take care of the institution that he always sent in a check from his business and a personal check to the Boys Ranch every month.

Author: Has that sort of thing happened more than once?

Bonnell: That has happened so many times. One year we (B.S.I.) decided to bring Norman Vincent Peale (to Albuquerque). He was an inspiration to me and to a lot of us and we tried to do business in a Christian manner. We scheduled a meeting for the convention center that would seat, oh, I think it's 2,400 people. We invited outside guests besides our stockholders. We rented a bus for the farmers and ranchers in Portales, etc. We filled the auditorium that year. Our official guests were the boys and entire staff of the New Mexico Boys Ranch. We limited the luncheon to five hundred people and put two boys or staff at each table. They got to meet a lot of people and it was great exposure. We did this around 1975 and again in 1977. Just one dividend out of that—a couple of years after that meeting one of our stockholders called me and said, "I've known you a long time and I know of everybody's keen interest in the Boys Ranch. We were lucky enough to be invited to those two stockholders' meetings and luncheons and Mama and I met four of those boys. We were so impressed and appreciated that so much that today we changed our will and left two million dollars to the Boys Ranch." Since that time he's changed the will again and left more. Glenda (Ted's wife) and I invited Mama and he down to the Ranch and we had supper with the boys. Mike gave us a great tour of the Ranch and those people saw the real Christian work being done and the results.

Author: It seems to me that the Ranch is on real solid financial ground today and is not going to have those financial troubles of years ago. What has made all the difference?

Bonnell: When I first got involved with the Board they were just operating it from the seat of their britches. Of course, their integrity and honesty goes without saying. But being a banker for years I had to say, "Look, we're handling public money and we should have a certified audit each year, just in case." I insisted that we develop some real rules and regulations that would conform not only with the Internal Revenue but with general practice of those kinds of institutions. Our holding company did have a trust company and that is how Rich Gregory got involved because he worked for us. We set up some trusts and we did all of this free for them for years. We were able to set up these trusts for permanent funds and set up procedures that are proper and fitting. It was a little costly for us at first to have to hire public accountants to come in and certify your statements. It seemed kind of ridiculous, but necessary.

Author: Your interest, your background in banking and your interest in procedure all came at absolutely the right time. It seems to me that the IRS wasn't all that happy with the financial accountability of the Boys Ranch. Things were a little sticky.

Bonnell: Well, the government has always given the Boys Ranch trouble. The Boys Ranch has never received a penny of government money for the care of any of the boys.

Author: But that's out of design?

Bonnell: Yes, but they still want to come and boss you and make you conform to every kind of rule and regulation. And they still look down their nose to Christianity being involved so deeply in an institution.

Author: Have there been any State Senators or Representatives that have been friends of the Ranch?

Bonnell: Well, Alice King and her husband the perennial Governor of New Mexico. Alice is a real Christian, as is Bruce, but she has taken a keen interest in the Ranch. Because of her and Bruce's influence they have been very beneficial to the Boys Ranch at various times with state government and with private industry.

. . . Another person I would like to mention is Mark Sloan, my pilot at B.S.I. and the corporate pilot. Mark was the biggest scrounger in New Mexico. A good many days when he brought me to Albuquerque (from Alamogordo) he'd spend his time out in the community, or other communities where our banks were, scrounging material and groceries, fertilizer, lumber and clothes for the boys at Boys Ranch.

. . . Our employees and Board members are responsible for building one of the dorms and the gymnasium, completed the barn, and we helped with the office, an infirmary and library. Our people donated the money, B.S.I. as a corporate entity never gave a penny.

Author: Who's the man that gave the large donation for the gymnasium and what was his interest in the Ranch?

Bonnell: Calvin Horn and he was on our Board, the B.S.I. Board. He's very interested in New Mexico. He has done a number of things for our state and charities. They had lost a boy in the Navy and they did this on his behalf. He gave forty thousand cash and the rest of us took up the slack.

. . . What B.S.I. did was to expose the boys and the Ranch and what they were doing to a lot of people. There's just been nothing I've ever done that's given me more inspiration and satisfaction as being involved with the Boys Ranch.

Author: Do you think that the Ranch could or should be larger?

Bonnell: I think they could be larger. But I think one reason that they have done so much good is that they know each individual. They know how and when to discipline them, to take care of them, to love them, and give them inspiration. I believe strongly in the way that they've divided the girls and the boys and the older boys over at the Ranch (Hart Ranch). I think that you can get too large in those institutions and they become institutions instead of people.

Author: With regard to the Ranches today, do you feel that there's still a need for such an organization?

Bonnell: Oh, there's the need today, even more than in 1950. The reason is that so many parents seem to feel no responsibility nor does their family feel responsibility for the kids. It seems like back in the older days that if something happened to a dad, the mother and the kids were taken care of by that family. Now, some people don't feel that responsibility anymore. There has always been a problem with liquor, but now the dope seems to have a more permanent effect. They just have their brains burned out and don't have sense enough to do anything.

Author: **Some of these kids are the tragic by-products?**

Bonnell: Yes, and even if their parents are at home, their brains are burned out. Those kids have to have the opportunity to be anything, to be a strong Christian and raise a decent family or to be President of the United States.

Author: **One final question. Does the Boys Ranch enjoy a good reputation in this state?**

Bonnell: Outstanding reputation! Everybody believes, without any exception, that it's probably the charitable institution with the best integrity.[30]

Story Five: JACK RATLIFF

John D. Ratliff, who has been called Jack all of his life, was born in a small eastern New Mexican town called Floyd on April 26, 1924. His parents were farmers/ranchers and Jack was educated in the public schools of Floyd. Jack has a degree in Latin American Studies from the University of New Mexico and a degree in Educational Administration from Eastern New Mexico State University. Jack Ratliff's interest in Latin American took him south of the border for fifteen years. Working for the Foreign Mission Board of Southern Baptist Convention Jack spent seven year in Honduras and eight years in Peru.

Returning to the States in 1966 he became the Executive Director of the Baptist Foundation for the State of New Mexico, a position he held until 1975 when he and his wife purchased the private Sunset Mesa School.

Author: How did you get involved with the Boys Ranch?

Ratliff: Well, I'd known about the Boys Ranch for a good many years before I became involved with it. Walker Hubbard was an old friend of ours from eastern New Mexico. When Walker retired, his assistant, Barry Morgan, came to me and asked me to help him with some of the problems they had. In order to do that I became a member of the Board of Directors and served from that time until now.

Author: Were you not Chairman of the Board of Directors at one time?

Ratliff: I was Vice Chairman, almost from the beginning of the time I was a member of the Board, that was in 1970. Then we reorganized the corporate structure of the Ranch and I served as Chairman for seven or eight years.

Author: What kind of financial shape was the Ranch in when you came on the Board?

Ratliff: We had no permanent funds and one ten thousand dollar CD at that time. There was a small amount of money in the bank. It was very, very close and the Ranch existed really with current fund contributions that were being received all along. That was all the money he had and fifty boys to feed. There was a debt that was carried over from back in the fifties, as I recall. It doesn't look very big now, but it seems to me it was in the vicinity of fifty thousand dollars or slightly more. I became Chairman of the Finance and Investment Committee. I was not active in the development. I was active in the investment and management of the funds as they developed and accrued over the years.

Author: So you knew Mr. Hubbard quite well?

Ratliff: Oh, I'd known him from the time I was in high school. We were personal friends. I had great respect for Walker. He was "Mr. Child Care in New Mexico."

Author: Was Barry Morgan really the man that ran the Ranch at that time?

Ratliff: Barry lived at the Ranch and did the day-to-day management. Barry was a good man. I'd known Barry all his life. His father and my father were good friends. Barry was so sensitive and gentle to a fault. He internalized the problems of the boys to the point that he couldn't handle it. And all of a sudden he either had to break or go, and he just left. It bothered me that I didn't realize what was happening to Barry. It wasn't a happy period as far as the Ranch was concerned. There were a lot of changes, particularly with the Internal Revenue Service, that we had to work through at that time, in both the restructuring of the corporation and the tax accountability of the Ranch to the IRS and to donors, this sort of thing.

Author: Did Morgan leave one day and Kull take over the next or was there someone else in charge?

Ratliff: It was almost that abrupt. We had no prior notice. All of a sudden he (Morgan) wasn't there and we had to move with somebody who was there and that was Mike.

Author: The early seventies were pretty dramatic!

Ratliff: There were several things at work. With the Tax Reform Act of 1964 the IRS became more sensitive. With subsequent years they were closing in on private foundations and the use of contributed funds. We were audited by the IRS. Fortunately for us, he (the IRS agent) was a friendly caring man because he could have closed the institution. He decided that the violations were not intentional. He gave (the Ranch) a period of time, less than a year, to reorganize and he almost dictated the terms of the reorganization.

Author: Time for change and restructuring?

Ratliff: It had to be done. That's when Barry came to me and said, "Jack, will you help me?" I said, "Of course, I'll help." I've never walked away when somebody needed help, particularly in child care. That's what got me involved, really.

Author: Could you recall some of the names of the new people that were brought on the Board?

Ratliff: Well, one who stayed on was J.B. Tidwell. J.B.'s one of the great men in the State of New Mexico. He and I have worked for the Boys Ranch and the Baptist Foundation for twenty-five years now. Bill Barnes was another. He was Chairman when it was reorganized. We had an attorney named Glass (Charles). He did the legal aspects of the reorganization and stayed on the Board as a friendly consultant for several years. Bob Davis was another. He stayed on the Board for five or six years. Jess May had prior relationship with the Ranch.

Author: How about Andy Sutter?

Ratliff: Let me tell you about Andy Sutter. Andy and I go way back. His father and my father were friends for years. Andy was a jeweler from Clovis. When Walker (Hubbard) took over the Boys Ranch it was bankrupt. They had no money. They had these boys and it was in a terrible condition. When Walker took over no one would serve on the Board because they had this debt and members assumed that they were going to be personally responsible for it. Andy's a Methodist by the way. And when he (Walker) told him about the Ranch and said, "Will you serve on the

Board," Andy did. In effect, he guaranteed the loans for the Ranch. He would have, I believe, happily lost everything he had if that's what it took to save the Ranch. He was so committed.

Author: Andy Sutter was one of the quiet heroes?

Ratliff: Yeah! Andy had a hard time with change because he was one of the old guys. Change bothered him because it was a threat to the financial stability we had and he had been the financial stability for fifteen to twenty years. We have great respect for Andy. He probably recruited more people from eastern New Mexico to support the Boys Ranch than everybody else combined. Andy stayed with us until very near his death. He's one of the great people!

Author: What's the biggest change that you've seen in the Ranch in the time period that you've been associated with it?

Ratliff: We moved from being a small single focus facility with a maximum of fifty-five boys at Belen; everybody living on campus and doing multiple services as houseparents and management people. We then moved to a facility with Families for Children, an adoption and a multipurpose agency, a girls' Ranch that we studied and worked on for ten years before it was born, and then to the Hart Youth Ranch over in Curry and Roosevelt Counties.

Author: So the whole thing is evolving?

Ratliff: Oh, it's growing and changing and it'll get bigger and more demanding. We're concerned that we constantly adjust the organization so that the integrity of the people and the happiness of the people is complimented by the organization. People have to be fulfilled in what they do and that's management's responsibility to see that they are.

Author: Has the personnel stabilized over the years?

Ratliff: We had excellent continuity in the management levels.
We're all concerned because houseparents burn out.
Turnovers are too high. Maybe eighteen months is the
average life of a house parent. I think these people are
highly motivated and we keep struggling to find a way to
do better and not have that high level of burnout.

Author: What is the funniest story you've ever heard of with
relation to the Ranch?

Ratliff: I guess I worked with the problems mostly. But thinking
back to Barry (Morgan) he made a practice of picking up
business people and he'd take them up in the Pecos
Wilderness somewhere on horses. One businessman
friend of mine who's from New Jersey was pure city.
Barry took him up in the mountains on one of these
outings. He would have given him (Morgan) any amount
of money just to get off of that horse and get out of there.
He never went again![31]

NOTES

1. Minutes Annual Meeting, January 26, 1970.
2. Minutes Annual Meeting, January 25, 1971.
3. Minutes Special Meeting, August 30, 1971.
4. Ibid.
5. Minutes Board of Directors, March 30, 1972.
6. Minutes Annual Meeting, January 29, 1973.
7. Ibid.
8. Minutes Board of Directors, July 20, 1973.
9. Minutes Board of Directors, January 28, 1974.
10. Ibid.
11. Ibid.
12. Newsletter dated July, 1974.
13. Minutes Board of Directors, May 16, 1974.
14. Minutes Board of Directors, January 27, 1975.

15. Ibid.
16. Ibid.
17. Ibid.
18. Newsletter dated October, 1975.
19. Minutes Board of Directors, January 26, 1976.
20. Ibid.
21. Newsletter dated August, 1977.
22. Newsletter dated April, 1978.
23. Newsletter dated October, 1979.
24. Ibid.
25. Ibid.
26. Ibid.
27. Interview with the Blevins Family, June 16, 1991, Clovis, New Mexico.
28. Interview with Billie Holder, June 18, 1991, Alamogordo, New Mexico.
29. Interview with Billy G. Barnes, June 27, 1991, Albuquerque, New Mexico.
30. Interview with Ted Bonnell, June 26, 1991, Albuquerque, New Mexico.
31. Interview with Jack D. Ratliff, June 25, 1991, Albuquerque, New Mexico.

Al Buck, Founder of
New Mexico Boys
Ranch, Inc.

The Al Buck Memorial states:
"BUCK KIWANIS MEMORIAL FOUNDATION
ESTABLISHED THIS HERD OF ABERDEEN ANGUS
CATTLE IN THE MEMORY OF

ALBERT E. BUCK
1903-1951
FOR THE PURPOSE OF FINANCIAL
ASSISTANCE TO THE BOYS RANCH"

Dedication of the first building located west of the highway
running through the ranch property.

Campus in the early 1950s showing the first cottages at Boys Ranch.

Dorothy and Walker
Hubbard. Mr. Hubbard
is credited with saving
the ranch from financial
collapse and recovery.
He served as executive
director from 1954 to
1972.

Aerial view of original campus in the late 1950s.

The Boys Ranch kitchen in the 1950s. The building was a surplus military structure brought in to serve as a temporary kitchen and dining hall.

Boys Ranch in the 1950s.

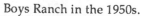

Hauling hay has always been a central part of the Ranch program.

Animal care is another important activity of Boys Ranch.

Early cottages included large bedrooms with bunk beds.
The residents shared a common bathroom.

The old "temporary" dining hall was remodeled numerous times
and was used until 1973.

Boys Ranch Residents in the 1950s.

Everyone on campus was called to mealtimes by the ringing of a bell located in front of the dining hall. The bell is still used today.

Boys Ranch staff and children in mid-1960s. The Boys Ranch bus was the primary mode of transportation until the mid 1970s.

Inside the cottage in the 1960s.

Construction of the
first modern cottage
completed with the
help of the boys
in 1969.

The modern cottages had bedrooms for two boys
and a bathroom for each 4 boys.

Overlooking the campus in the early 1970s.

A day together in Albuquerque in the mid 1970s.

The swimming pool was constructed in the 1950s and covered for year-round use in 1986.

The gymnasium was constructed in 1976.

The campus in the early 1980s.

New Mexico Girls Ranch was opened near Santa Fe at Lamy in 1982. This cottage was the first structure at Girls Ranch.

Modern cottages included a kitchen and dining room to create
a more family-style atmosphere.

Girls Ranch Residents and staff in 1994.

Families for Children, the foster care and adoption agency was added in 1982. This picture shows the 1st administrator and current employees at the 10th Anniversary celebration in 1992.

Hart Youth Ranch near Melrose was donated by Beulah Hart Miller for the purpose of providing a home for children. The program opened a new cottage for older boys in 1984.

The Hart Youth Ranch
program was established
in 1984.

Branding Day
at the Hart Youth
Ranch in 1994.

Winners at the Annual Boys Ranch Rodeo in the late 1980s. Boys Ranch, Girls Ranch, and Hart Youth Ranch residents compete for trophys each year.

Boys Ranch residents and staff in 1994 in front of the 1st cottage built on ranch property. The building has always been referred to as "up top."

Chapter Six
THE RANCH EXPANDS AND REACHES OUT

The election of Ronald Reagan as the 38th President of the United States was the signal to many Americans that a new era had begun. For the staff, donors and friends of the New Mexico Boys Ranch the new era was announced by Mike Kull in an editorial entitled "Turning Point." Kull wrote as follows:

> In an effort founded largely in faith, the Boys Ranch Board of Directors and Advisors recently voted to make a bold effort in New Mexico. Alice King, a member of our Board of Advisors for the past six years and New Mexico's First Lady, has agreed to assist the Boys Ranch in building a Girls Ranch.[1]

Kull went on to say that, "The Directors and Advisors also decided to pursue the building of a satellite Boys Ranch on the Hart Ranch south of Melrose as per the wishes of Beulah Hart Miller, who bequeathed the land to the Boys Ranch."[2] Thus, two brand new outreaches were proclaimed as the new decade began.

GIRLS RANCH

August 1, 1981 was one happy day when a group of people gathered in a piñon meadow southeast of Santa Fe near Lamy to formally break ground for the new Girls Ranch. Jack Ratliff, President of the Board of Directors, took charge of the ceremony which included Governor Bruce King. The Governor spoke appreciately of all who had worked to bring the Girls Ranch into existence. Alice King, the Governor's wife who had chaired the Girls Ranch Advisory Committee, gave words of appreciation to the following groups: to Amrep Corporation for the gift of 117 acres of land; to the Kerr Foundation for the $75,000 matching grant to get the program rolling; to the Architect Richard Yates for donating the architectural plans; and to the Public Service Company of New Mexico for installing electricity at the site.

One year later, the first building was nearing completion and the first girls were in residence for the start of the 1982-83 school year. Thanks to a $200,000 matching grant from the Mabee Foundation of Tulsa, Oklahoma the new Girls Ranch program was off to a fine start. Al and Norva Lue Davenport and their own three daughters along with twelve new girl residents made history as the first occupants. Life was obviously pretty crowded that first year as other buildings were being constructed. One young girl was quoted as saying, "It's like the Partridge Family moving in with the Brady Bunch."[3]

By August 1983 three modular buildings were moved on campus, set on foundations, hooked into utilities and stuccoed. With the Davenports moving into one of these buildings it became the Manager's Residence. The two other buildings became staff housing and the administrative office. With the completion of the second girls cottage the new campus was becoming established. The site even took on a more urban look after the Santa Fe High School F.F.A. planted evergreens, built a terrace, and sodded a lawn donated by Green Chaparral Turf Ranch.[4]

A wide variety of civic organizations, especially women's groups, came to the aid of the Girls Ranch during the early 1980s. These included the Delta Kappa Gamma Society, the Rio Rancho Ranchetts, Epsilon Sigma Alpha, The New Mexico Federation of Women's Clubs, the Tanoan Country Club, the Cosmopolitan Woman's Club of Albuquerque, and of course the New Mexico Cowbelles who had aided the Boys Ranch for years.

HART YOUTH RANCH

The history of the Hart Ranch reads like a true chapter out of a western novel. Oasis is the best word that some have used to describe the heart of this piece of land south of Melrose in eastern New Mexico. Massive cottonwoods shelter the ranch headquarters and at their base lie cool fresh water springs. Through the centuries wild animals, Plains Indians, army soldiers, cattle barons and ranchers have all taken a respite in this cool shade.

Lonnie Horn was probably the first man to stake a claim to this prairie oasis. He and three partners secured the vast acreage for open range ranching in the 1880s. When his partners sold out, Lonnie kept his portion and proceeded to building his ranch headquarters in this grove of trees.

It is fascinating to note that the vigas for the original building came from the old Pete Maxwell house in Ft. Sumner. This is the house that the noted outlaw Billy the Kid (William Bonney) was killed in by Sheriff Pat Garrett on July 14, 1881.

In any case, this ranch was originally called the Pig Pen Ranch because Lonnie Horn's brand was four crossed slashes resembling a pig pen (#). Local lore has it that the Horn family employed the best cook in the area named "Pig Pen Annie." At one time in history the nearby town of Melrose was called Brownhorn for Walter, "Wildhorse" Brown and Lonnie Horn. Later when the AT&SF Railroad selected Brownhorn as a site for their repair shops they laid out a town site and renamed the place Melrose.

After Lonnie Horn's death in 1903, Mrs. Horn sold the Pig Pen Ranch to Frank Divers who then sold it in 1908 to Charlie S. Hart, a former cowboy turned businessman and rancher. Eventually, Charlie Hart put together seven ranches totaling over two hundred sections. (A section normally means one square mile).

Hart had two sons by his first wife, Charles S. Hart Jr. and Jere D. Hart. After his first wife's death Charlie Hart remarried May Morris who had a little girl named Beulah May from a previous marriage. When Mr. & Mrs. Hart passed away, Beulah May inherited "the home ranch." Later she married her ranch foreman, Bob Miller, who was a well thought of local cowboy. In her will, Beulah May left this magnificent historic tract of land to the Boys Ranch. While not specifically stated in the will, it was known that various members of the Hart family, in addition to Beulah, desired that the Hart Ranch be used to help children from troubled backgrounds.[5]

After several years of planning, during the summer of 1982 the old Hart Ranch was upgraded and prepared for use. Stan and Brenda Henderson, former houseparents at Boys Ranch, made the move across the state to care for the ranch and the cattle that were being moved there. Slowly, the old ranch headquarters was being renovated.

By the winter of 1984 the first building at the Hart Youth Ranch, as it was being called, was under construction. The new building was identical in design to a new building being constructed simultaneously at the Girls Ranch. It was designed to accommodate ten to twelve boys and one houseparent couple. The building utilizes a passive solar heating system and was made possible by the generous gifts of Marion Wooton of Melrose, and Waunette (Collins) Shore of San Jon, N.M. and her two sons. (Mr. and Mrs. Al Collins of Colorado Springs, Colorado, and Mr. and Mrs. Jim Collins of Tucumcari, N.M.) A bronze plaque of Wayne Collins was permanently displayed in this new building.

FAMILIES FOR CHILDREN

The third new outreach program that started in the 1980s was called Families for Children. It was the result of a six-year struggle to get the state to pass Senate Bill #189 titled "Child Placement Act." This act authorized child care agencies such as Boys Ranch to have their own Foster Care Programs. The task of getting this new foster care and adoption agency up and running fell to Bob Hoeberling. Having founded and directed the Christian Center Counseling Service in Albuquerque in 1973, this talented man from Michigan faced unique challenges. The goal and primary purpose of Families for Children was to place children from Boys Ranch and Girls Ranch in private homes when they have no viable home situation to return to.

By the summer of 1982 Hoeberling had recruited and trained the first foster parents and this new outreach was ready to begin the placement of young boys. By the end of that first year, nine sets of foster parents had been trained and girls were included. Seventeen homes, mostly in Albuquerque, were licensed by the summer of 1983 and a Families for Children Auxiliary had been formed. Recognizing the awesome and delicate assignment of placing children, the FFC Auxiliary engaged in monthly prayer meetings for the decisions that were being made.

Three years after its creation, Families for Children was providing the following services: foster placement in private licensed homes; adoption placement for children and families that qualified; adoption services for infants and toddlers on a very limited basis; emergency foster placement and specialized foster care, aftercare and follow-up for children returning home.[6]

With all of the new activities and programs occupying so much time and energy during the 1980s, it is important to remember that life went on at the original Boys Ranch. In fact, one of the special features at the Ranch needs our attention. Because with some fifty boys to keep, it became a very important task to take time twice a year to check each boy's progress. During this time of critical evaluation each individual boy is examined for progress. It is when each boy's strengths are pointed out and encouragement is given to improve his weaknesses.

Every single aspect of each boy's life is considered during these sessions, including his educational progress, his health needs and his behavior at school and church. Every person important in that boy's life is involved. This includes the boy's parents or guardians, his houseparents and those who work with him on the Ranch. Even the boy is asked to evaluate himself. Sometimes this turns out to be the most valuable insight. (This is now done at all three ranches.)

Through the early 1980s, Nikki Kull, the Boys Ranch Social Worker, arranged the time schedule and kept the entire process moving. Pat Trembly, Director of Cottage Life, led the evaluation team, tied the information together and made formal conclusions. A Plan of Service was drawn up at the end of each session which specified the goals for the boy and his needs in the program. Over the years this evaluation procedure has become a very valuable part of the Boys Ranch program. It enables the parents to be involved, gives the boy specific goals and helps the Ranch to meet the needs of each boy.[7]

In April of 1984, under the leadership of Executive Director Mike Kull, the Foundation for Boys Ranch and Girls Ranch was developed. The specific goal of this new endeavor was to build an endowment to sustain the work of the organization for years to come. As planned, all endowment funds were and continue to be fully invested with only the interest being expended. This basic but crucial fact assures dependable income for the programs year after year after year in perpetuity.[8]

With this new program in place, Seminars on Wills and Estate Planning were established and staffed by Mike Kull and Rich Gregory, an Albuquerque resident who is both a CPA and an attorney. Both Gregory and Jeanene Ondrick were elected to the Board of Directors at the June 30, 1983 meeting. At the same time, officers for the year were elected as follows:

President	- Jack Ratliff of Albuquerque
Vice-President	- Clovis Evans of Artesia
Secretary	- Arno Romero of Belen
Treasurer	- Barbara Nicholson of Belen.

It was the first weekend of September in 1984 when a large crowd of folks from around the state gathered at the Boys Ranch to celebrate forty years of continuous service. Emceed by Frank Haley of KOB Radio News (Albuquerque), speakers included: former superintendent, Barry Morgan; Fred Flowers, a boy rancher from the late 1950s; John McCarty, a man involved in the early development; and a recorded message from Senator Pete Domenici. Two longtime board members, J.B. Tidwell and Andy Sutter, were recognized and made remarks about the Ranch. Twelve-year old Sean Hilverding, who was a Boys Ranch resident, closed with a heartfelt prayer that ended . . ."and, Dear God, help us to be the people we should be."[9]

It was safe to say that both the staff and the Board of Directors welcomed this joyful celebration. When it was over they rolled up their sleeves and proceeded into another new decade of work.

New and significant faces were appearing at the Boys Ranch. When the Tremblys moved to the Hart Youth Ranch, Don and Laura Hawes filled in as managers until the right couple could be selected. That special couple turned out to be Phil and Marilyn Gregory. Both Gregorys are graduates of John Brown University and both hold Masters Degrees. The Gregorys had been employed by the Belen School District prior to arriving at Boys Ranch.

The winter of 1985 was so severe that four times the winter rodeo planned for the Boys Ranch was canceled due to bad weather. The rodeo was finally held, as was a ski trip to Sandia Peak, a "not so nice" all-day horseback ride which ended in the rain, hikes to La Drone and Black Mountain, pizza trips, tree trimming, and firewood cutting. For most of the boys the highlight of that winter was the car show in Albuquerque and the chance to see Boss Hogg and "Kitt" from the television series Knight Rider. However, for one young man at the Ranch the high point of the season was when he proudly announced that he was a "father." His pet sow had just had a large litter of piglets.[10]

Thanks to Marvin Broce Construction Company and a lot of assistance from the State Highway Department, the Girls Ranch went into the winter with a new one-and-one-half mile paved road into the campus. What a blessing this was over the frequently impossible muddy road of previous years. Gifts from the Albuquerque Woman's Club, Rio Rancho Ranchetts, the Cowbelles, and the Federation of Women's Clubs combined to make these girls feel really special.[11]

Over at the Hart Youth Ranch that winter the Clovis Eagles Club came to the rescue with a big powerful portable welding rig to aid in the construction of a new corral. Previously this same club had provided most of the pipe and cable for this project as the ranch slowly became a more functional working ranch. The nearby Melrose Public School was beginning to feel the impact of the Hart Youth Ranch as four out of five of the first group of boys became involved with the school basketball program.[12]

On June 1, 1985 the Hart Youth Ranch officially celebrated its grand opening. Over two hundred guests from all over New Mexico, Colorado, and Texas attended. The reason for the one-year delay of this celebration was due to heavy rains which made the road to the Ranch impassible. As any visitor to the Ranch can attest, the site is not exactly an urban location.

With the official opening of the Hart Youth Ranch, the major expansion effort was basically complete. Now with more children and more staff, Mike Kull and Charles Gibson were able to turn their attention to two major concerns: long-term financial security and quality programming. To accomplish this task, organizational changes were made. Kull became President of the Boys and Girls Ranch Foundation as well as President of the Boys Ranch Organization. Gibson became Executive Director and an officer of the Board of Directors.[13]

Change was coming in other areas as well. Billye Coey became the first full-time Social Worker Counselor at Families for Children.[14] Billye had a Masters Degree in Counseling from UNM and had previously worked with foster homes and adoption placement. As a special assignment, she was to begin work with the Albuquerque Crisis and Pregnancy Center working with unwed mothers. By late fall FFC had placed eleven children into permanent adoptive families and twenty-nine children had received temporary Christian foster care.[15]

Unfortunately, the other change that spring was not so pleasant. Andy Sutter, a longtime friend of the Ranch, died suddenly in Clovis. Andy was first elected to the Board of Directors in 1956 when Boys Ranch almost closed due to financial problems. Andy was the Treasurer for many years, and never grew tired of telling how he was the Treasurer when there were no funds, only debts. In 1980 Sutter's first wife passed away and with his substantial gift the Dorothy Sutter Cottage was completed and dedicated on December 7, 1982.[16]

The Boys Ranch has historically been a very nonpolitical entity which has gone out of its way not to seek government funds of any kind. However, from time to time as the years went on various state agencies, especially the Department of Human Services, tried to bring the Ranch under their control. It needs to be clearly understood by all that throughout the years the Boys Ranch has always worked hard to establish statewide standards for child care. With this in mind, the attempt in 1985-86 by the Department of Human Services to piggyback their regulations on top of the Health and Welfare Department regulations was fought by both the Boys Ranch and all other members of the New Mexico Christian Child Care Association. State legislators were flooded with thousands of letters of protest which served as the catalyst for legislative support. Eventually, both the New Mexico House of Representatives and the Senate were instrumental in prohibiting the two departments from proceeding with their plan. With this political victory in hand, the Boys Ranch and others pushed for permanent improvements in the law defining the relationship of the Department of Human Services and private children's homes. With aid from Representative Gary King, Ron Gentry, Senator Stuart Ingle, and many others, House Bill #435 passed overwhelmingly. Governor Carruthers signed this bill into law on March 16, 1987.[17]

The previous year Boys Ranch began proudly displaying the seal of the Evangelical Council of Financial Accountability on all of its envelopes and newsletters. What this meant was that this national organization required all members to meet and maintain rigorous standards of accountability. The purpose for the Ranch was simple. It was just one more way that the credibility and trustworthiness of the entire organization could be demonstrated to friends and the public in general. Donors to the Boys Ranch have always been looked on as special friends working together with the staff in helping children.[18]

The New Mexico Christian Child Care Association selected the Boys Ranch as the first facility in the state to go through its Peer Review Process in the fall of 1986. The comprehensive standards consisted of almost 200 regulations covering all aspects of child care programs, including fiscal accountability, personnel practices, organization and administration, grounds and equipment, fund raising, and the program itself. At the end of 1987 there were only three New Mexico organizations certified by the high standards of ECFA. The Boys Ranch was one of them. Given the media attention to corrupt television evangelists, it was crucial for the Ranch to remain the epitome of integrity.[19]

Springtime means graduation time to students everywhere. At the Girls Ranch the graduation service at Santa Fe High School in 1986 was especially meaningful. What made it special was Sharon Brown. For you see, Sharon was the very first girl to arrive at the Ranch. In many ways this tall lanky blonde girl from Farmington symbolized through her growth the growth of the Girls Ranch. During her high school years she lettered in volleyball, served as president of the student body and was in a wide variety of activities. Just weeks after her graduation she was involved in a serious auto accident which placed her in intensive care for weeks. In spite of the painful recovery, Sharon entered Eastern New Mexico University. The following summer she received an internship in Senator Domenici's office in Washington, D.C.

Less dramatic, but just as important, was the 1986 graduation from Melrose High School of Bryce Yancy who was the third of five brothers who had come to the Ranch in 1976. The following year Kent Smith, a graduating senior from Boys Ranch, was honored at a ceremony where he received the highest rank of the Boy Scouts, an Eagle Scout. Not to be overlooked is the fact that year after year children of various staff members excelled in their respective schools and went on to successful careers. For example, in May 1987 Kevin Gregory and Cyndi Davenport both graduated. Both sets of parents are Ranch Administrators and both students were outstanding in their schools. These and many other graduates are living examples of what time, love, and care can accomplish in young people's lives.

The summer of 1986 saw the much-needed enclosure for the swimming pool at Boys Ranch completed. The 3,608 square foot building is made of glass, cinder block and aluminum. The south and west walls have sliding glass doors and the roof has panels which can open in warm weather. Gifts from Perry Stevens of Texas, Sandia Foundation, McCutcheon Foundation, and the Martin Estate provided the materials. Under the leadership of Don Hawes, Cottage Life Supervisor, the staff and boys of the Ranch put in hundreds of hours of labor on this project. The result is a wonderful year-round swimming pool.

Airplane accidents have played a tragic part of the Boys Ranch's history beginning with the demise of founding father, Al Buck. His early death almost cost the Boys Ranch its future. Additionally, at least one building on campus is named in honor of a young man who lost his life in an airplane. To this grim list was added the name of Albert J. Mitchell in the summer of 1986. Mitchell was killed when his single engine, private plane crashed for unknown reasons near Mosquero, New Mexico. Mitchell had been a longtime friend of the Ranch and at the time of his death he had been a member of the Board of Directors for eighteen years. A permanent memorial fund was established at Boys Ranch in his honor. The Mitchell legacy lives on through his oldest son "Scooter," who serves as a Director, and his wife Jeannette Mitchell, who serves on the Advisory Board, thus becoming the third generation to do so.[20]

A more cheerful note was the successful completion of the new dining hall and multipurpose building at the Girls Ranch. This newest construction project became a real challenge when the matching fund grant of $140,000 only allowed seven months in which to raise the money. Fortunately, friends came through with the funds and the building was completed. It includes a unique kitchen which was specifically designed to process and store food for use on the Ranch.

As the two new ranches grew there was a direct attempt to link them together in more than just an administrative sense. For example, the three ranches have paid visits to each other. They have gone to the Cliff Hammond's Amusement Park together, and to baseball games, and to the annual Harvest Party at Girls Ranch. The cooperation has also seen "whirlwind" work trips like the time when forty-three boys and twelve staff members from Boys Ranch spent the day cleaning, cutting wood, and taking down old fences at the Hart Youth Ranch. Through exchanges like these, all of the various residents are made to feel like they are part of the larger family of God.[21]

When Bob Hoeberling left the Families for Children outreach for a new challenge on January 1, 1987, he left behind a fully established foster care agency. From a very small beginning foster care placements had been provided to some fifty-one children and twenty-one children had been placed in adoptive homes. Families For Children had already approved licenses to twelve families and counseling had been provided to more than seventy parents.

Replacing Hoeberling at FFC was Billye Coey who had been with the agency for over a year. With a Masters Degree in Counseling and eleven years of teaching experience, Coey was well prepared for her new role.[22]

After a number of years of prayer, research, and planning the New Mexico Boys Ranch and Girls Ranch Thrift Store opened its doors across from the fairgrounds in Albuquerque. Al Humble, the former business manager who had been replaced by Brian Stevenson in 1983, took on the responsibility for this unique money maker. The grand opening was held on June 6, 1987 with Barbara Gatzweiler becoming the first full-time manager. Perhaps the cruelest irony of all was that valuable time and energy had to be expended in order to keep an adult bookstore from sharing the same building and parking lot. Sometimes it is indeed a strange world. By 1989 the second thrift store opened its door in a renovated building in Las Cruces.

Executive Director Charles Gibson introduced the readers of the Ranch newsletter to the new administrators at Girls Ranch in the winter of 1988 as Bert and Brenda Schrader of Arlington, Texas. The Schraders had previous experiences with church camps and conferences, food service management and public relations. They also came to Girls Ranch with the experience of having worked with numerous foster children from troubled backgrounds.[23]

Unfortunately for the Schraders, they had hardly settled in before a major setback occurred at the Ranch. For on May 1, 1989, fire destroyed the maintenance building on campus. While a large number of tools and supplies were lost, no one was injured and a nearby building was not destroyed. Ironically, one of the projects underway at that time was improvements to the water system which would provide for fire hydrants and hoses on campus.[24]

As the Boys Ranch organization paused on September 2, 1989 to celebrate its Forty-fifth Anniversary Reunion, all involved had much to be thankful for. Not only was the organization more financially secure than ever in its history, it also had a good idea of where it was heading in the future thanks to a diverse group of forty-four people who spend hundreds of hours strategizing the future. Everyone was involved from houseparents to secretaries, administrators to bookkeepers. The result was a clear-cut 50th year plan and a strong vision of what could be done for children and families in New Mexico.[25]

Story One: MOZELLE TREMBLY

Mozelle Trembly was born on August 3, 1940 in Carlsbad, New Mexico, and graduated from Carlsbad High School in 1958. A number of years later she went to work for Thiocal Corporation in Roswell. It was here that she met and married Pat Trembly. Pat had grown up in Gallup and just graduated from Eastern New Mexico University. This young couple were both involved in the educational training of Native Americans for industry. Some five years later, in a Nixon administration cut off of funds, this unique program was terminated and both Tremblys were laid off in March of 1974.

Following a chance encounter with Mike and Nikki Kull, who Pat had known at ENMU, an opening for houseparents occurred at the Boys Ranch. They accepted the position and made the move in June of 1974. Pat and Mozelle spent ten years at Boys Ranch, six as houseparents and four as administrators. As the expansion came, the Tremblys became the first Ranch Administrators at the Hart Youth Ranch in 1984. They remained in that position until November 1990 for a total of sixteen-and-one-half years of service. (Stan and Brenda Henderson were the first

Ranch Managers when Boys Ranch took control. Ray Hall and Jim Riley were early boys at Hart Ranch who graduated from Melrose High School.)

Author: How many boys were at the Boys Ranch when you went there in 1974?

Trembly: We were licensed for fifty, but tried to keep the number at forty-eight. The youngest was five years old.

Author: What kind of kids were they?

Trembly: They were hungry for love. Hungry for acceptance. Boys who the first night upon our arrival began telling me horror stories. We had one pair of twins and I mentioned that I'd never be able to tell them apart. One of them pulled his shirt collar aside and said, "Well, you can always tell me by these scars." I said, "How did you get those horrible scars?" He said, "My mother threw me through a window!"

. . . One little Navajo boy from up north came to us in the middle of the night. Charles (Gibson) had called and said, "Have a bed ready for this boy. He's been in jail for a week." This is an eleven-year-old boy that we're talking about. He had been found in an abandoned car after sniffing paint. He had passed out, been in a coma and then in the hospital for a number of days. His family wouldn't or couldn't claim him. He arrived in the same dirty paint-covered clothes that he had on when he was picked up. For days he was scared and absolutely frightened to death. He was a very quiet, very shy boy who stayed about four years.

Author: Do you remember the big yellow school bus?

Trembly: We all hated it. In the summertime it was so hot the children were antsy and rowdy by the time we'd get to church. The big boys would pick on the little boys. The vans came much later.

Author: Did you ever have runaways?

Trembly: Yes, occasionally. Once we had two boys that hid under the seat of the school bus. When the boys got to the compound they just left and fooled around town all day. Of course, we were frantic. We called their step-parents—nothing. It was fine, because they came home on the bus thinking that they had gotten away with the whole thing. It certainly ruined a day off for me.

Author: You and Pat became quite involved with five brothers right?

Trembly: Yes. Randy was five, the youngest, when they came. Chris was almost seven. Bryce must have been nine. Scott was ten, and Rex twelve. (What followed was a tragic story of a separated father and mother, a wayward mother, a father that couldn't stay off the bottle and the complete breakup of the total family.) Eventually, Rex graduated from Belen High School and Scott ran away. Bryce and Chris moved to the Hart Youth Ranch with us in 1984. Bryce went on to college at ENMU. (Chris was killed in a terrible accident several years after leaving the ranch.)

. . . Chris Sandoval is a real success story. He was one young undisciplined child. When Charles (Gibson) brought him to us he said, "This is a kid who's ruled the roost where he has been." In fact, Chris never started school one year simply because he didn't want to go. As it turned out, what he needed was a father role model in his life. He was so eager to love and be accepted. Years later he was one of the first boys to move into Belen in the semi-independent living area. He now has a college education, a reponsible job, is married and has two beautiful daughters.

Author: You were the first administrators at the Hart Youth Ranch; right?

Trembly: Yes, in 1984 when Pat and I moved over there the old ranch headquarters had not been renovated. At one point we made snowballs from the snow that came through the doors in that old ranch house . . .We had rattlesnakes come right up to the back door, lots of prairie rattlers.

Author: **How many boys went with you and Pat? And what was it like?**

Trembly: There were six in the beginning. Several came later. We knew and loved the boys and we learned a lot from our neighbors. Cowboys came from the other ranches to help us. Everybody wanted to see who was going to run the Hart Ranch.It was an exciting time. About eighty head of cattle came with the Ranch and others were soon donated (actually the original herd was trucked there from the Boys Ranch). Mike (Kull) had initiated a deal at cattle sales that the ranchers could use their gift as a charitable donation. We'd have hats to give away and it would be a matter of pride with those ranchers to walk out of the Boys Ranch sales day with one of those caps on.

Author: **Did you have other livestock?**

Trembly: Oh yes, we had gifts of about twenty horses, chickens, turkeys, rabbits, and at one time a little herd of sheep. The coyotes got all my ducks and geese, eventually all the little sheep. There are a lot of coyotes still there.

Author: **Any special story?**

Trembly: Right away Shawn comes to mind. He was seven or eight when he came to us. He never knew the day that he came to the Ranch that he was going to be left by his mother. It came as a real shock. Today he is married and is a college student. He's just very intelligent with lots to offer and has just really covered great strides in dealing with his back ground.[26]

Story Two: TOMMY TUCKER

He was born Tommy Lester Tucker on August 2, 1948 in Hobbs, New Mexico. After a family divorce, Tommy's mother had trouble supporting the family. With the support of J.B. Tidwell, Tommy came to the Ranch at age fifteen. After high school, a hitch in the Army, and a seven-year truck driver job, Tommy and his wife, Darlene, moved to Boys Ranch in 1971. Tommy Tucker today serves as the Farm Manager at Boys Ranch.

Author: **What was your first recollection of this Ranch?**

Tucker: I was fifteen when I came in 1963, just before John Kennedy got killed. My first recollection was, "How do I get out of this place?" It was desert, barren and I'd lived in town all my life. When I first came here there was twenty-five kids in each building, some as young as five. There were three old quonset huts that I remember.

. . . Barry Morgan and me hit it off. He was super. In fact, I think that's where the Ranch started turning me around. I could look him right in the belt buckle and tell him anything (Morgan is 6'6" tall).

Author: **Did you do a lot of work?**

Tucker: You didn't leave the kitchen until you had a chore. I drove the tractor a lot to irrigate or chop weeds or whatever. That's where I learned to work.

Author: **Did you eat well?**

Tucker: We did. We always ate good. We had our own milk cows which we all took turns milking. No pasteurization. We took whole milk, strained it, put it in the refrigerator and cooled it, and the next morning we drank it. When we had to pasteurize we scrapped the milking project. It was like

fifty thousand dollars to buy the equipment and we didn't
have it. It was cheaper to buy the milk. For a while all we
ran was Black Angus on this place.

Author: What is that weird looking cow I saw out here?

Tucker: You're talking about Whatsi the Watusi from Africa. A guy
gave that rascal to us. We could sell his head for a trophy.
He has got a six-foot head span. A lot of people think he's a
Texas longhorn.

Author: What's the most unusual thing they have ever tried to
raise?

Tucker: Chinchillas. Morgan had them in a boxcar. I think they
lost their shorts on those chinchillas. (Actually they were
all donated.)

... We've had up to sixty horses, but that is too many.
They eat a lot. Most of what we get are used-up racehorses.

Author: Do the kids that come here know what a Ranch is all
about?

Tucker: They have no idea. We have more fun with kids from town.
You tell them, "Open the gate." So they open the gate and
you drive through. "Now close the gate." Invariably, after
they get the gate closed, they will be on the wrong side of
the fence. It's more fun. Just watch them and see how long
it takes them to figure out which side of the fence to be on
after they get the gate closed.

Author: Tommy, you came here as a street-wise kid! Are these
kids today like that?

Tucker: These kids have no imagination. When I was a kid, if they
cut us loose to do something, you'd go jump in a ditch or
dig a cave. There was a lot of things you could do. But the

kids nowadays, all they know how to do is sit in front of a TV and play a Nintendo.

Author: **When you were in high school, did the kids get along in Belen Schools?**

Tucker: No. We had us the Spanish-American Revolution back in '65 or '66, one big gang fight between the Ranch and the town. One of our guys ended up getting stabbed right in school. Man, the police came and one kid went to jail.

Author: **Did you meet your wife in school?**

Tucker: Just after I got out. She was working at the Tasty Freeze. I'd tell her to put green chile on it. (Hamburger) I found out later that when she was mad at me she'd put lots of Tabasco sauce and lots of chile on it. That was just how I liked it and I thought that she was really being nice to me with all that stuff. It made her mad because I'd sit out there in the car and eat my hamburger and smile at her.

Author: **Did you ever serve as houseparent?**

Tucker: Yeah, five or six times. Every time somebody would move out of a building, I'd have to move in. They burn out pretty fast. Five years is a good average. We've had some last three days.

Author: **Tommy, since you're a product of the Ranch and you've seen it change over the years, is there still a reason to have a place like this?**

Tucker: Definitely! There's still a lot of bad parents out there. If we had the money, we could put five hundred kids in here and still have people trying to get in.[27]

Story Three: JESSE MAY

Born in Brownfield, Texas on September 29, 1922, Jesse A. May spent his younger years in Clovis, New Mexico. Jesse's family and Andy Sutter, previously mentioned, go back a long way. When Andy was a young boy in Clovis, he worked for Jesse's father and hung around their watch store. Andy Sutter worked for Jesse May's father for a number of years and eventually was responsible for getting Jesse interested in the Boys Ranch. After graduation from Texas Tech and a stint in the U.S. Army as an engineer, Jesse May moved to Farmington, New Mexico in 1953 and has operated a very successful jewelry business ever since. Jesse May spent over thirty years on the Board of Directors of the Boys Ranch.

Author: How and when did you first hear of the Boys Ranch?

May: I had heard of it over the years and had heard of Walker Hubbard. Seems they had picked a man from Farmington to be on the Board, but he never went to a meeting. So Andy Sutter called me and asked if I would serve on the Board. That was about 1956 or 1957. I had a very small store then, so I would have to drive down and spend the day and drive back. No interstates then.

Author: As an Easterner, these distances in New Mexico just boggle my mind!

May: But we drive faster! In those days the roads were not good, but we still drove sixty to sixty-five miles an hour all the time. Never had an accident.

. . . When I got on the Board the Ranch had no credit. They couldn't even go buy a loaf of bread on credit. They owed everybody in Belen and the people in Belen didn't think much of Boys Ranch . . . We tried to make the decisions, tried to give directions, and we went into too much detail.

We had a big Board, fifteen to twenty out of the twenty-seven. We'd sit around in the lobby of the main building for our meetings. Holm Bursum and Bill Barnes spent years as the leaders.

Author: **Was there ever a time when you thought that you should become a United Way agency?**

May: Yes, we tried that in Clovis and it hurt. It really hurt the amount that we got from Curry County because Andy (Sutter) had a real following over there. That was probably in the late '60s or early '70s. Our whole budget was probably fifty thousand. When we expanded into the Girls Ranch and the Youth Ranch, that's when our budgets really went up fast. But by that time we were on good financial ground. We have always been extremely conservative. We really have been very careful.

Author: **Would you say that the reputation has improved over the years?**

May: It's just snowballed. The reputation has improved and the quality of life of the children has improved. We could really use a Ranch up here in this area (Farmington).

Author: **Were you on the Board when the Hart Ranch was given?**

May: Oh, yes. I'd known the old parents years ago. Andy Sutter, bless his heart, was a go-getter and knew how to talk people into things. He kind of convinced these folks that since they didn't have any heirs it'd be good if they would leave that ranch to the Boys Ranch. As I remember, there was a large mortgage on it and we ended up selling off a portion, maybe three thousand acres or so to pay off the indebtedness. It's all clear now.

. . . One of the problems when we started in Melrose was we were afraid that we'd just swamp their school, because it's so small, if we moved twenty-five boys in there.

Author: I understand that the school has really welcomed them.

May: Oh, they have really been pleased with the boys. It helped all their sports. It's been a great thing, a real marriage between the town of Melrose and our Ranch.

. . . Have you heard about the Air Force wanting our land down there? In fact, we had an awful time swapping with them. It's (the Ranch) right near the Melrose bombing range from Cannon Air Force Base so the Air Force wanted part of the Ranch. They (the Air Force) went out and bought land on the other side of the Ranch so the Ranch now has that. (The Ranch sold the Air Force an easement and the state leased the Ranch some of the land within the bombing range.)

Author: Were you involved with the decision to start Families for Children?

May: Yes! Charles Gibson came up with that idea. We could see the need. There's so many unwanted children and so many families wanting children.

Author: What makes it any different than any other adoption agency?

May: One is that we're real particular that they're Christian homes. We try to train the would-be parents. If we get a girl that wants to put a child up for adoption, we do everything we can to help her. Just the whole concept of doing it right.

Author: Hasn't it been kind of difficult for you, living so far away from the Boys Ranch, to convince people here in Farmington that they should be interested?

May: It hasn't been too hard. My church (Presbyterian) gives a
         lot, especially the women's organization. It's their project.
         They give clothes and toilet articles like toothbrushes and
         cold cream, and food. You know, I have had a lot of the oil
         people help us here. For example, used pipes. I've gotten
         miles of pipe and miles of cable to make fences. Lots of
         pickup trucks donated. One time Arizona Public Service
         was building a big power plant west of Farmington and
         they gave me all their scrap wire, copper wire. We had to
         bring a big semi-truck up from the Ranch to haul all the
         wire back. We sold that copper (wire) for four or five
         thousand dollars.

Author: Do you see a need for the Ranch today like when you
         first went on the Board?

May: I think probably more. We have more unwanted children
         today then we've ever had. More abused children than
         ever. We need more satellite organizations, but the more
         you expand the more problems you face in having the
         organization the way you want it.[28]

Story Four: MARGARET GIBSON

Margaret Gibson did not have your average typical childhood. She
was born and raised in Tangankika, British East Africa, of Lutheran
missionary parents. By 1963 East Africa had become the new nations of
Tanzania and Kenya. Margaret experienced schools in both nations. Her
first eight years were at Augustina School in Tanzania and then at Rift
Valley Academy in Kenya. Margaret and her brothers and sister all
graduated from Rift Valley Academy. At first the trips home were by the
old British East African Railroad. Several years later, the two-hundred
mile trip was by bus and became a major border crossing. Margaret
described her childhood to this author as "idyllic." She said, "It was a
wonderful time to be in Africa." Margaret came back to the states first to
Wheaton College and then graduated from Columbia School of Nursing

in New York City. Margaret and Charles Gibson were married in a ceremony in which all fifty boys from Boys Ranch participated. For their honeymoon, friends and the employees at the Boys Ranch collected enough money to send them on a trip to Africa to visit Margaret's parents.

Margaret: You know New Mexico is just like the central province of Tanzania where I went to school. Sparse vegetation. Not truly desert, but not a whole bunch of water. The big blue skies. It made me feel right at home.

Author: Were you hired as a nurse?

Margaret: No, a wife! Wives shared their husbands' salaries in the mid-'70s. (Later Margaret had her own salary.) We were sort of a package. Then they built the clinic. Nikki Kull's brother, Max, who is with the UNM School of Medicine, knew that they needed elective sites for medical students in family medicine under supervision. By 1979 we had four or five medical students down here one afternoon per week all year so they got to know the kids. We called it a health maintenance program.

Author: Did that include the staff?

Margaret: Yes, and even the folks down the road that wanted to bring their kids in.

Author: Do these kids have a lot of health problems?

Margaret: No. I just marvel at that! We deal with what I call "well children." We just don't see much illness. If anything gets missed, it's teeth. We do see kids that come here little, like a twelve-year old who'll be eighty pounds. There just wasn't enough milk and protein going in them. We'll see fat kids come in and we don't do anything about putting them on a diet, but six to twelve months later, by virtue of

Boys Ranch lifestyle (no nibbling—not a lot of junk food) these kids grow and sort of firm up. Kids leave here much healthier.

Author: **Do you deal with abused kids?**

Margaret: Yes, and our doctors and medical students are very sensitive. They are really tuned-in to our kids and have a real rapport that I've been thankful for . . . I think that we have gotten pretty good at knowing "this is significant and this isn't significant."

Author: **Any unusual circumstances?**

Margaret: We've never had a rattlesnake bite. Two cases of appendicitis. Several farm accidents. We had a tractor and trailer run over a boy. The boy did fine. I don't know what he did to the trailer. Very tough kid. I would have to say that God has been merciful.

. . . Boys Ranch is epidemiologically an interesting place because of the farm, the population (seventy people living together), and its rural with farm machinery. It's a place where, potentially, you could have anything in the area of accidents or illness and it doesn't happen. We've done everything that we're supposed to keeping kids immunized and checked for TB.

Author: **Are all medical expenses picked up by the Ranch?**

Margaret: Yes, we have coverage with Blue Cross/Blue Shield. If we had one rich benefactor who said, "What could I do?," it would be orthodontics.

. . . Today we are seeing kids who have greater psychological needs than ten or twenty years ago. We have been fortunate at Boys Ranch to be able to use a school psychologist who is wonderful.[29]

Story Five: CHARLES GIBSON

Charles Gibson's relationship with the Boys Ranch is nothing short of amazing. He arrived at the Ranch as a widely traveled unemployed "free spirit" and left the Ranch as Executive Director to go to theological seminary.

Charles was born on June 13, 1947 in San Angelo, Texas, the son of a Presbyterian minister. At age eleven, the family moved to La Junta, Colorado where Charles graduated from high school in 1965. After one year at the U.S. Naval Academy, he decided that the military life wasn't for him and transferred to Adams State College where he graduated two years later. After a short stint of teaching school, he spent six months touring South American with his sister. His job experiences included: the Office of Economic Development in D.C., the buying and selling of exotic automobiles, a business venture on the island of St. Croix, a catering business in Washington, et cetera. Within the next few years of his life, Charles had experienced a major motorcycle accident and the disappointment of a cheating business partner.

Author: Tell me how you ended up at the Boys Ranch?

Charles: I stopped in Belen to visit my brother and got involved
           with a Christian group that he was with. Two guys, one of
           which was Bob Hoeberling who started our Families for
           Children facility, wanted to start a retreat center. They
           rented the old house at Boys Ranch and I moved there to
           help clean it up. It was just totally trashed out. That was in
           early 1972. By April, I was living there. I slept out on the
           front porch and ate in the dining hall. Barry Morgan was
           always open to the "unorthodox" (Charles laughs). The
           retreat center never happened and I just got more and more
           involved with the staff and kids as a volunteer. When Mor-
           gan quit in 1972, Mike (Kull) asked me to work for him. I
           just said, "Okay, I'll work for you for one year." I was still
           kind of a free floating spirit. I started driving the bus, then
           working in the store and pretty quickly Mike just started

depending on me for more and more. At that time I went
on salary. We were both about the same age, both had high
ideals. We both loved the Lord. It seemed like we really
understood how the other thought and we developed a
very close relationship.

Author: Were you ever in charge of the Ranch?

Charles: I became assistant superintendent. Eventually I concen-
trated more and more on development work. I was never
a houseparent. Later, after I was married, my wife and I
would take care of buildings. I did a lot of public speaking.
That sort of came natural for me. I began going to Board
meetings.

Author: You've seen lots of changes in the Board?

Charles: I remember when the Board of Advisors went from being
a retirement Board of old Board members to being like a
training ground.

Author: Did you strive for representation?

Charles: Yeah! If anything, it became more focused on getting people
on the Board who were Christians. We were hiring more
and more Christian people to work here because this was a
Christian work, but it wasn't officially a Christian work.
We changed the Charter to make it that. The words "religious activities" were included in the incorporation purposes. We became officially Christian. After that we were
able to say openly, "Well, we are an organization that's
helping children, but we are a Christian organization."

Author: Has this increased the giving?

Charles: Yes, yes. It became a selling point for the Ranch, the fact
that we did not take any government tax money. We could

say to people, "Your tax money does not support us."
People would say, "Well, they deserve our support."

Author: Do you take government surplus equipment and food?

Charles: Surplus equipment like they make available to schools. We get commodity food through Roadrunner, an organization that gets food from any source and makes it available to charities at ten cents a pound.

Author: Where does the largest amount of your budget come from?

Charles: For quite a while we were very proud of the fact that most of our money came from people who made small contributions and it wasn't the "fat cats" who supported Boys Ranch. That's still pretty much true, but the difference now is that we have a small group of generous donors—four or five hundred who give a tremendous portion of the money that runs the Ranch. We have a core of really committed donors who carry a disproportionate share in their generosity. There are people who write their checks for over ten thousand dollars each year.

Author: Let's talk about the major changes that you've seen in your twenty-odd years at the Ranch.

Charles: Size! Earlier we had forty-two. We got to where we could handle fifty here and Girls Ranch and Hart Ranch. We basically had two to three times as many.

Author: Staff?

Charles: It's increased probably four to six times.

Author: Budget?

Charles: It's gone from like just under two hundred thousand to just over two-point-two million. Just the cost of living has increased a lot, and the quality of care has increased dramatically. What we're doing with children now we used to just dream about doing. It's quite a different program.

Author: If someone asked you what is the single biggest change you've seen in twenty years, what would you say?

Charles: The kind of kid that we're helping! When I first came here the boys were basically what might be termed "pre-delinquent." They were pretty tough kids. They were older. You just hoped that you could contain them and control them. They were older, harder kids. These are younger kids. We have been able to get them earlier. That has been the most significant change that I can think of as far as what would affect our success. Because, of course, if you can get them younger you have a much better chance.

Author: Any such thing as a boy hero to come out of Boys Ranch?

Charles: There's a number of boys and girls who've done very well. Bill Bailey comes to mind. He was here in the early days and went on to college and became a helicopter pilot. He was in the Desert Storm Operation. Chris Sandoval (previously mentioned) and Sharon Brown (previously mentioned). There are quite a number that have done well. We don't have super achievers, but we have had many gratifying evidences of kids who've gone on to build and sustain quality relationships; who have started and raised families; who have been responsible citizens; who have reached out and cared for others.

Author: What do you see as your biggest frustration over twenty years?

Charles: It's frustrating that we weren't able to get more of the Christian community involved. There's a general apathy on the part of the Christian community to actually do some

things to help kids. I feel that the Christian community
needs to be doing a lot more practical intervention in
people's lives and could be making a real difference, but
we just don't see that.

. . . I think that there's a tremendous need for this kind of
operation. Families are hurting all over the country. Speaking as Charles Gibson, I think that we need to find alterna-
tives for that child before they are removed from the home.
That would take family therapy, family counseling. And
then the ones we brought here would really need to be
here. But that doesn't impress people as much because they
don't see the buildings.[30]

NOTES

1. Newsletter New Mexico Boys Ranch, October, 1979.
2. Ibid.
3. Newsletter N.M.B.R., July, 1983.
4. Ibid.
5. Dedication Ceremony literature, June 1, 1985 and various
    N.M.B.R. Newsletters.
6. Newsletters N.M.B.R., July, 1983 and October, 1983.
7. Newsletter N.M.B.R., Fall, 1981.
8. Newsletter N.M.B.R., July, 1984.
9. Newsletter N.M.B.R., October, 1984.
10. Newsletter N.M.B.R., March, 1985.
11. Ibid.
12. Ibid.
13. Newsletter N.M.B.R., July, 1985.
14. Ibid.
15. Ibid.
16. Ibid.
17. Various sources including Ranch newsletters and interviews
    during the 1980s.
18. Newsletter N.M.B.R., March, 1986.
19. Newsletter N.M.B.R., July, 1986.

20. Ibid. It is tragic to note that Ted Bonnell, Mark Sloan, Jack Scroggins and Calvin Horn all had sons killed in plane accidents.
21. Newsletter N.M.B.R., October, 1986.
22. Ibid and Newsletter N.M.B.R., February, 1987.
23. Newsletter N.M.B.R., Winter, 1988.
24. Newsletter N.M.B.R., Spring, 1989.
25. Newsletter N.M.B.R., Fall, 1989.
26. Interview with Mozelle Trembly, June 1, 1992, Roswell, New Mexico.
27. Interview with Tommy Tucker, May 24, 1992, Boys Ranch.
28. Interview with Jesse May, June 8, 1992, Farmington, New Mexico.
29. Interview with Margaret Gibson, May 31, 1992, Boys Ranch.
30. Interview with Charles Gibson, May 24, 1992, Boys Ranch.

CHAPTER SEVEN
Into the Nineties And Beyond

As the decade of the eighties came to a close, the Boys Ranch paused on September 2, 1989 to celebrate its 45th anniversary. Over six hundred people enjoyed a day filled with fun, food, and fellowship. It was a day to renew old friendships and to explore first hand the labors of forty-five years of struggle and hard work. One of the tangible results of this gathering was the desire to form an alumni association. Others, believe it or not, started to lay plans for the 50th anniversary to be held in 1994.[1]

Earlier that summer some twenty-one boys were returned to their parents and twenty-one new ones took their place at Boys Ranch. At the conclusion of the school year, over one-half of the Boys Ranch residents were on the Ranch scholastic honor roll—the highest number in history. Thirteen of those same boys qualified for the regional cross-country meet in Denver where one of them, Robbie Wright, qualified for the nationals. A generous donor made possible the purchase of large commercial washers and dryers to the delight of Mela Torres, the long-time laundress. Even the dining hall got a new look with brand new tables, chairs and carpeting.[2]

Undoubtedly, for the residents of Boys Ranch, the really "big shock" of 1988 was the Bernardo earthquake of November 28th. The epicenter of the quake was just eight miles from the ranch and measured 4.7 on the Richter scale. There was some "rocking and rolling," but no major damage. In fact, it wasn't long before T-shirts appeared on campus proclaiming, "I survived the great Bernardo earthquake."[3]

As the decade changed, Girls Ranch started a new 4-H program which demanded a year-round commitment from the girls involved. The love and trust displayed by the animals to these girls plus the sense of responsibility required combined to make this a valu-able new venture. The efforts of these girls paid off at the Santa Fe County Fair where they sold their animals and won six different prizes, including second and fourth place for showmanship.

At the Hart Youth Ranch, the old decade ended with the completion of a number of projects, including the building of a hay barn. This
barn turned out to be an illustration in stewardship. "The poles came
from Melrose, the metal supports from Hobbs, the lumber from Gallup,
and the tin from Albuquerque. The padwork was donated by John
Eastwood of Clovis. The boys from Hart Ranch, with help from Girls
Ranch, tore down the barrier part of a drive-in movie theater and
salvaged the metal. The residents and staff gave their labor. They were
not only building a hay barn, they were building character."[4]

As it turned out, 1989 was a year of important legislative activity in
the area of child care. The Adoption Act was changed to make the
adoption process move more quickly and smoothly. In addition, a bill to
license social workers was modified to promote quality social service
without arbitrarily disqualifying valuable current workers.

The Adoptive Family Service League, dedicated to mutual help, and
the ministry of Families for Children developed COACH (Caring for
Others Who are Adopting Children). The purpose of this new venture
was to pair off couples who are waiting to adopt with couples who
have already adopted. The goal was to help the prospective parents
through this traumatic time. Each month during 1989 saw an average of
nine to thirteen children in foster care.

By this time, the Families for Children staff was developing a statewide reputation for excellence in the field of foster care and adoption
training. That ability was recognized when FFC administrator Billye
Coey was selected in 1990 to serve on The Governor's Task Force on
Adolescent Pregnancy.[5]

At the same time, Mozelle Trembly of the Hart Youth Ranch was
invited to present a workshop session at the Southwestern Association
of Executives of Homes for Children (SWA). Her workshop was entitled
"Houseparents and Their Own Kids." It explored problems and solutions
for couples who are raising their own children while being houseparents. This is no small task which down through the years various
ranch administrators have mastered.

1990 was a challenging year for New Mexico Boys Ranch, Inc.
During the year, there were sharp budget cuts. While contending with
financial reductions, a very careful focus on priorities kept the services
for children at the same level. With extra staff effort the number of

children helped was not reduced at all. At the same time, there was an extended effort made toward preparing for the future. The first steps toward the 50th year plan began in operational meetings which involved virtually all staff members.

During 1990 a total of 153 children were cared for in the following programs:

> Boys Ranch - 79 boys; Independent Living Program - 6 young men; Girls Ranch - 28 girls; Hart Youth Ranch - 11 teenage boys; Foster Placement - 18 children; and Adoption Placement - 11 children. The average length of stay for children who have left the ranch during the year varies as follows: Boys Ranch - 18 months; Girls Ranch - 21 months; and the Hart Youth Ranch - 21 months.[6]

Other statistics produced during 1990 revealed that the Permanent Memorial Funds had become a major source of income. A total of one hundred twenty funds totaling $703,463 produced an income of $66,932. Another program of very special value is called Partners. These are people who have pledged to give monthly gifts to help the children. This small group of special donors actually covers a significant portion of the costs incurred each year. During 1989-90 some four hundred eighty-eight Partners contributed $180,155.[7]

An unfortunate personal loss occurred at the end of 1990 when after sixteen years of dedicated service to the Boys Ranch, Pat and Mozelle Trembly resigned as administrators at the Hart Youth Ranch. Over the years they had worked in a variety of positions from houseparents for the "little boys" to administrators. In every instance, they gave 100% effort to their job. However, two tragedies broke their hearts. In 1989, their oldest son, Mike, was killed in a tragic accident in Albuquerque. Then in September 1990, Chris Yancey, a boy the Tremblys had raised from childhood, was killed in a motorcycle accident.

Replacing the Tremblys were Mike and Becky Howell, formerly of Boys Ranch Town in Edmond, Oklahoma. Coming with Mike and Becky were their two boys, Josh and Chris. Also coming to the Hart Youth Ranch from Oklahoma were Elvin and Diana Long who were to be the new houseparents.

Meanwhile, over at the Girls Ranch, the challenge was twenty girls enrolled in six different schools. This soon became eleven schools. While each girl was encouraged to be involved in her school and in the extra curricular activities, it sure kept the staff hopping or should we say "driving." To help ease this problem as well as to provide education tailored to the individual girl, the Girls Ranch soon opened its own on-campus school. It was a happy day when a girl named J.B. won first in showmanship and had the Reserve Grand Championship Steer at the Santa Fe County Fair. Four other girls won awards at Santa Fe and seven boys won awards at the Valencia County Fair.

On July 27, 1991 Hart Youth Ranch celebrated its tenth anniversary by dedicating its new vocational-agricultural building. The funds for this new versatile building were provided by Lee and Mildred Merrill of Clovis. The building is designed for the ranch boys to learn mechanical, welding, and woodworking projects. At the same time, the Eagles Club of Clovis donated the funds necessary for a half-court of basketball.[8]

Then on September 28th the Girls Ranch held their dedication service for the long-anticipated enclosed swimming pool. Prior to that happy event, the Girls Ranch had held their first ever Parents Day in which seventeen out of twenty families participated. Christmas dinner 1991 was made very special for the girls by having a Christmas dinner at the Governor's Mansion with Governor and Mrs. Bruce King.

After six years of service to Families for Children, Billye Coey left the agency to pursue other vocational interests. Coey had first joined FFC in 1984 as a case worker. During her tenure she had set high standards of training to prepare parents for their new children. Coey initiated The Adoption Orientation Seminar for prospective adopting couples. In addition, she served on various state task forces and was involved with a number of legislative issues with the Adoption Coalition. Nikki Kull graciously stepped in as the Interim Administrator to keep things running smoothly.[9]

Statistically speaking, 1991 was another year of growth and heal-ing for over one hundred and fifty children. The breakdown was as follows: Boys Ranch - 71; Independent Living - 6; Girls Ranch - 23; Hart Youth Ranch - 16; Foster Placement - 16; and Adoption Placement - 19. These figures, great as they are, pale in that for every eight children referred for help only one could be accepted. In all, there were some three hundred eighty-two referrals for residential care in that one year

alone. Fortunately for New Mexico Boys Ranch, Inc., some five hundred and five Partners generously gave $221,385, thus helping to meet
the annual budget of $2,092,960. One year later the number of Partners
had risen to five hundred and forty-five and their gifts accounted for
$252,911. Of additional significance is the fact that in 1992 one hundred
and sixty-eight Permanent Memorial Funds produced some $59,941.66
in needed revenue.[10]

In retrospect it seems ironic that in the Winter 1992 issue of The
Corral (Ranch Newsletter) Executive Director Charles Gibson wrote a
column titled "The Bottom Line: Did We Make a Difference?" Of course,
he was asking what the long-range effects of the program would be
on the children. However, considering the fact that shortly thereafter
Charles announced his own resignation, the question has to become
rhetorical.[11]

For twenty years Charles and Margaret Gibson had worked to
improve the "bottom line" at Boys Ranch. Charles had served seven
years as Executive Director and was instrumental in the development of
the four divisions of the organization. For two decades he had
administered the direct mail fund raising of the organization. Margaret helped start the weekly clinic program at the Boys Ranch shortly
after her marriage to Charles in 1976. Each of the Gibsons' four children
were born during their stay at Boys Ranch. After considerable reflection,
Charles made the career decision to enter seminary at Regent College,
British Columbia.

In world history 1991 will long be remembered for major political
restructuring, such as the break-up of the Soviet Union. Ironically, major
restructuring was occurring within the Boys Ranch at the same time.
Over the years the organization had expanded and so had the
responsibilities of each position. Also, the Ranch had expanded the
demand for increased accountability on all levels.

Recognizing the need for professional help in solving these and
other problems, the Ranch hired the consulting firm of Alston-Kline, Inc.
from Seattle, Washington. Files were scrutinized, aptitude and personnel tests were given and every aspect of the organization was examined
from top to bottom. Within the Ranch a task force known as The
Administrative Policy Review Committee worked through the process
of strategic planning. The final result of this self study was the complete

reorganization of the entire Ranch administration. In a well thought out extensive plan, the bylaws were rewritten, the Board committees were reorganized, and the corporation structure was flattened out.[12]

Today the Boys Ranch operates based on the following major committees.[13]

> **Foundation Board (Investment Committee)** - Purpose: Serve as the governing authority over The New Mexico Boys and Girls Ranch Foundation and ensure it effectively accomplishes its stated purpose.
>
> **Agriculture Committee** - Purpose: Provide agricultural expertise and assistance in producing profits from the agricultural assets of the corporation.
>
> **Finance Committee** - Purpose: To ensure that the corporation is in good financial condition and in compliance with generally accepted accounting standards and government mandated reporting.
>
> **Program Committee** - Purpose: To ensure Board member awareness, involvement and support in all program activity, human resources and new program development.
>
> **Development Committee** - Purpose: To ensure Board awareness, involvement, and support in all development planning and activity of the Ranches.
>
> **Nomination Committee** - Purpose: To ensure The Board of Directors is fully staffed with qualified, competent and well-trained members.

Administrative restructuring triggered other personnel changes in 1992-93. The newly created position of Executive Vice-President of the Foundation was filled by Patrick A. Fort. Born on November 4, 1950 in Carlsbad, Fort holds graduate degrees in both mechanical engineering and law. His previous experience as both assistant district attorney and then county attorney for Dona Ana County make him a valuable counselor for The Boys Ranch Foundation.

Ronald Gloetzner was hired as the new Vice-President for Programs.

Gloetzner was born in Detroit, Michigan, and prior to coming to Boys Ranch he had served as a juvenile court officer. Gloetzner had additional experience as a chaplain at a juvenile detention facility.

Other administrators added during the reorganization include Susan McAndrew - Vice-President for Development; Tom Taylor - Vice-President for Finance; and Nikki Kull - Vice-President for Human Resources.

At the Hart Youth Ranch, Don and Donna Ashby became the Administrators. The Ashbys came to the Ranch from Carlsbad, New Mexico where Don had worked for the past ten years with the Bureau of Land Management as the supervisory range conservationist. Don has a degree in Range Management from New Mexico State University, Las Cruces. Donna operated a day care center for children in her home while living in Carlsbad.

Overseeing all the ranches as the new Agricultural Manager was Steve Patton. This Clovis native has a degree in agricultural economics and is responsible for all the agricultural planning, budgeting and management. It is hoped that his skills will help improve the agricultural development of each ranch.[14]

The last set of statistics available prior to the 50th anniversary reveal that in 1993 a total of one hundred and thirty-two children were cared for in the various programs of New Mexico Boys Ranch, Inc. Broken down that figure shows the following:

Boys Ranch - 65; Independent Living - 5; Girls Ranch - 31; Hart Youth Ranch - 16; Adoptive Placement - 3; and Foster Placement - 12. In addition, three adoptions were mentioned and sixty-two birth parents were counseled for both adoption and foster care.[15]

During 1993 the ages of residents ranged from eight to eighteen. At Boys Ranch the average age was 13.9; at Girls Ranch it was 15; at Hart Youth Ranch it was 16; and at the Independent Living Home it was 17. The average boy stayed at the Ranch for 16.8 months; the girls stayed 17.7 months; and the youths stayed at Hart Ranch 10.6 months.[16]

Through very careful management once again the Ranch operated within its fixed budget. For 1993 that budget was $2,433.703. Thanks to the five hundred and fifty-four Partners who pledged monthly gifts some $275,838 was received. An additional $48,606 was received as income from the one hundred and eighty Permanent Memorial Funds. However, the largest single income continued to come from the thousands of small donors and various organizations who in 1993 contributed $1,673,453. This fantastic support is due in no small part to the honesty and integrity of the entire Ranch operation. All financial records are audited annually and the Ranch proudly displays the seal of the Evangelical Council on Financial Accountability. Additionally, the Ranch is certified by The New Mexico Christian Child Care Association and is licensed by the State of New Mexico.[17]

Reading the Annual Report one is struck by the fact that a great deal of time was spent planning for the future. The Ranch Mission Statement was rewritten as were all the bylaws. Every ranch and agency also dreamed their dreams of the future.

At the Boys Ranch plans were being laid for the building of a "special" fifth cottage. Currently being called, The Transitional Living Cottage, Phil and Marilyn Gregory dream of the day when some six to ten boys can be trained in the skills of self-sufficiency before reentry into the real world.

At the Girls Ranch the staff, under the leadership of Bert and Brenda Schrader, were also planning for an independent living house. A home in Santa Fe would help ease the burden of commuting to and from the Ranch, especially in the winter. On the dream list also is the thought of a third dormitory for another ten or more girls.

Over at the Hart Youth Ranch plans were being laid by Don and Donna Ashby and others for a new General Purpose Building. This future building would serve both as classrooms and for indoor recreation. Add to that the need for a library, additional corrals, an arena, an Arts and Crafts Center, and someday a second cottage, and you are looking at their future.

In Albuquerque, at Families for Children, administrator Ron Gloetzner and his staff were laying plans for recruiting and training more foster parents. By providing temporary homes away from the ranches, numerous children could share in a small family environment. As Gloetzner said in the Winter 1994 issue of The Corral, "Children are the hope of the Future, but the Future is Now for many and we won't have another chance . . . ."

THE YEAR OF JUBILEE

"And you shall hallow the fiftieth year
and you shall proclaim liberty throughout the land
to all its inhabitants.
It shall be a jubilee for you."
Leviticus 25:10

Fifty years is a long time. It is a long time for an individual, for a church or for an organization like the New Mexico Boys and Girls Ranch. It is also very biblical, for in the Old Testament it is the final year in a cycle of fifty years. In the book of Leviticus it is called the Year of Jubilee and it is even mentioned in the Dead Sea Scrolls.[18]

Historically, the Year of Jubilee in effect provided for a general overhaul of the economic and social life. It was meant to restore persons and property to their rightful conditions. Land was to be returned to its original owners and slaves were to be set free. It was meant to be a kind of new beginning, sort of a point in time when all who had failed to maintain their place in society were given a chance to start over.[19]

As the Ranch prepared to celebrate its Fiftieth Anniversary, employees paused to reflect on the biblical message contained in Leviticus. Several of the concepts appeared to be both timeless and appropriate. First was the concept of returning to one's family and roots and the renewing of relationships. Second was the concept of renewal. Everyone needs to reflect on their blessings and to renew their hearts. The Ranch has come through a decade of major growth and expansion. There is the need to tie up loose ends from the past and to start anew. Finally, there is the need for a vision of the future.[20]

In sharing his vision of the future, Mike Kull reflected on the philosophical message of Bill Gothard, the well-known Christian Seminar leader. Gothard's thesis, according to Kull, is that basically every organization must die before it can live, and that every vision must die before it can live. Kull believes that the Ranch which was started with grand and noble plans almost died, that the Ranch went through a period of trials and tribulation, and that out of that struggle came a corporate perspective of their mission.[21]

Kull went on to explain his view that if the corporation does not grow, it will start to die. "If we try to hold onto a concept of what Boys Ranch was in 1970, we'll die. Kids aren't the same as they were in 1970 or 1960. The family is going through tremendous changes. We have to change with those changes both as a society and as a corporation."[22]

Further discussions with Kull revealed his deep understanding and concern over the changing nature of the Ranch donors. It appears that the average donor is now over sixty-five years of age, and it is obvious that they are not going to be around forever. While no donor can ever be taken for granted, the challenge for the Ranch comes in how to appeal to a younger generation. It is a very complex financial and economic situation which will require a great deal of attention. Mike Kull expressed it quite well when he said:

> It's going to be a challenge to keep a balance between our Christian values and the needs of our society. How far to go in being responsive and caring and compassionate to bring people in, and yet not selling our values out. It's like life, it's just constant monitoring and constant changing.[23]

It appears obvious to those people closest to the Ranch that God has brought them this far for good reason. Their times of tribulation have not been in vain. This organization is well prepared for the unfinished work ahead. Revival and renewal are the order of the day. Let the trumpet of the Lord sound for God's people await the future.

Story One: J.B. TIDWELL

Jonas Benton Tidwell was born in north Texas in the town of Westminster on August 16, 1914. His father was a minister and for the first fifteen years of young J.B.'s life they moved every single year. Arriving finally in Lovington, New Mexico in 1929, J.B. finished high school there in 1931. Moving to Hobbs in 1935, he married a local school teacher named Maggie Jordon. J.B. carries a lot of the early history of Hobbs around in his head. Things like, the first oil well was developed in town in 1929 and is still producing, the railroad came to town in 1930, and the fact that the streets were still unpaved in 1935. It is interesting to note that as a young person J.B. went to school with members of the Hobbs family for whom the town is named. J.B. Tidwell is the ultimate consummate member of the Board of Directors having served since the mid 1950s.

Author: How did you first hear about the Boys Ranch?

J.B.:   I was helping Walker Hubbard with an estate that had been given to the New Mexico Baptist Children's Home. I was the liaison man between that ranch and the Home. When he (Hubbard) was asked to help the Boys Ranch, he started getting new board members and he asked me to serve.

             . . . I remember his (Hubbard's) funeral. It was just like a homecoming there with a lot of children who had been at the   Children's Home. You see, Mike Kull was raised at the Baptist Children's Home so he knew from first hand how to operate. He was the administrator of the whole organization until he became President of the New Mexico Boys Ranch Foundation.

Author: What do you remember about the finances when you came on the Board of Directors in the fifties?

J.B.:   I remember sitting at the first board meeting and Mr. Hubbard talking about the lack of credit. He'd gone to one of the banks to establish credit and to try to give some authenticity to our ability to pay bills. He encouraged the directors to ask others to contribute so that we could get the Ranch back on its feet. He continued to lead in that area being very careful about purchases and trying to stay within a budget. We're still operating that way. Our budget this year (1990-91) is almost two million dollars and we're spending within 5% of the budget. So we're living with our budget.

Author: What were your first impressions of the Ranch?

J.B.:   I didn't know what to think. The land looked poor to me.
            The manager lived up on the hill and he kept some of the
            children there. That's where we had our Board meetings.
            We had a meager start!

Author: Did the boys do all of the work?

J.B.:   The boys did the best they could with all different types of
            duties. They would work in the kitchen, in the dining room,
            out in the fields and they would rotate. Eventually we got a
            laundry and the boys would work in the laundry. They
            baled hay and raised a good many vegetables at that time.

Author: Were you involved in the selection process of how these
            boys got to the Ranch?

J.B.:   We depended on the staff for that. However, if a boy at
            Hobbs was in trouble and someone called us, we'd get in
            touch with the management. I have taken boys to the Ranch
            at different times after they were accepted. We have some
            that came through local law enforcement agencies. Tommy
            Tucker lived in Hobbs and their family situation wasn't
            good. We took them both (a brother) to Boys Ranch. Tom-
            my made it and his brother didn't. Tommy stayed through
            high school. We sent him to industrial school and now he's
            in charge of all the tractors, trucks, trailers, et cetera. He
            lives there, enjoys living there and we're so grateful . . .
            One of the things that's been good for me is the young men
            that come in here after they have left (they) just want to say
            "thank you" for what you did for us. A young man from
            Eunice came in not so long ago and said, "I'll always be
            grateful."

Author: Have particular civic organizations been really active in
            their support?

J.B.:   I'm glad to say that the Kiwanis Clubs of New Mexico wanted it to take hold. The New Mexico Cosmetologists and Hairdressers took the Boys Ranch on as a project and have continued to support it for years. The ranchers wives, called "Cactus Cowbelles" continue their support. The New Mexico Federation of Women's Clubs have been very active. The Delta Kappa Gamma Society of the teachers have had an interest. We have support from so many different areas.

Author: As a board member, how did the decision get made to start a Girls Ranch?

J.B.:   There was found to be a need for girls. We would have calls, but we didn't have a place for girls. Our Ranch Board could see a need, particularly Alice King who has been on the board for a long time. She and Bruce (the Governor) did a wonderful job in helping develop and finding a place for it. She had a lot of help from other members, but she was the main push. They contributed financially to it, and lent a lot of support.

Author: How about the Hart Youth Ranch?

J.B.:   We had a family that desired very much to help the Boys Ranch. We started off with probably ten thousand acres but had to sell off some land to pay the indebtedness on the Ranch property. We wound up with fifty-nine hundred acres. Our attorney has been a great help, especially with the Foundation. The Foundation is what is empowered with the handling of the funds and doing all the buying and selling of properties. They handle the DARE property that's been given to the Boys Ranch.

Author: What's that?

J.B.:   It was a drug rehabilitation program in Albuquerque and they got to the point that they couldn't operate it. They offered it to the Boys Ranch with the stipulation that the funds from it would always be used for the youth of the Albuquerque area. We're selling some of it back to the city and the money will go into a trust fund.

Author: Has the Foundation been a success?

J.B.:   It has been a great success. Our assets now (1991) are about seven million dollars. This is intended to help by giving income to the operation of all the divisions of Boys Ranch from the interests or earnings on the Foundation funds. It is now contributing about $180,000 a year to the operation of the New Mexican Boys/Girls Ranch.

Author: How did the Ranch get into the thrift shop business?

J.B.:   Al Humble conceived the idea because we were given so many things that we couldn't use at the Ranch. People were so willing to give away things that could be sold at a thrift store. It became profitable the first year and I hope it continues even though it may be over the break-even point. People have been so willing to give.

Author: What's next?

J.B.:   That's all part of our Five-Year Plan, you know. An all-year swimming pool (now complete) at the Girls Ranch. We need to rebuild the storage area that burned a couple of years ago. We need a place to handle our woodworking, metal working, and welding shop to keep the Ranch going. We lost a lot of our tools and equipment. That building needs to be rebuilt and that's one of the priority projects at this time.

Author: I see the need everywhere. It seems to me that there are literally hundreds of these kids that need help. Is it possible to expand?

J.B.:   We have been studying the feasibility of increasing our
             capacity at Hart Youth Ranch for the older boys. The boys
             there seem to do well in school. They're liked in the com-
             munity, they become a part of the community. They're able
             to have a six-man football team at Melrose because of our
             residents there. It required a good deal of investment to
             start up and then investment each year.

             . . . We try to do a quality job with the young people we
             have. There is a lot more demands for new donations now,
             and so consequently we've got to be wise in our planning.
             I think our executives, Charles Gibson, Mike Kull, and their
             staff have been very frugal in their operation. And we con-
             tinue to plan that way. We hope to serve more, but we want
             to do it in a quality way. Once we take a young person, we
             want to be able to stay with them as long as needed.[24]

Story Two: NIKKI KULL

Born in Clovis, New Mexico on May 21, 1947, Nikki grew up in
Portales close to the Baptist Children's Home. Her family were neighbors of Walker Hubbard. In fact, Nikki's back yard actually bordered on
the Children's Home property. In what could be called a real-life
"backyard romance" Nikki and Mike became acquainted, went to Portales
High School and then on to Eastern New Mexico University. Married in
1968, this young couple moved to Carlsbad where Nikki taught school.
In what this couple considered a "vision" they ended up at the New
Mexico Boys Ranch as houseparents in December 1970.

Author: What was your first impression of the Boys Ranch?

Nikki: The trees had lost all their leaves. It was deadly brown. I
           thought I was at the end of the world; the wind was blow-
           ing; it was cold. We ate supper that night in the old quon-
           set hut with lots of rowdy kids. There were gaps around
           the windows. It was a very, very crowded, very noisy
           atmosphere. If you got up from your chair, somebody

behind you had to scoot up closer to their table so you could get out. That's how we ate for four years. The kid across from me bit into his fried egg sandwich and yolk ran down his face . . . I thought, "I'm not sure I can do this . . ."

In our home the tile on the floor was black, but most of it was chipped up and there were chunks out of it everywhere. I felt like I was really on the mission field big time. There was a round cone-shaped couch in the center of the floor. And about this time one of the boys came through riding his bicycle and started riding it around this couch. I looked over at Mike and said, "Do I have to put up with this kind of thing?" And he said, "No, you can tell him to take the bicycle outside." That's how green I was. I didn't know how much control we had over the kids. I was only twenty-three and the oldest kids at the ranch were eighteen.

Author: How many boys would have been there then?

Nikki: There were sixty boys at the Ranch and twelve in our building. Mike and I and Barry Morgan and his wife and the farm manager and his wife were all that worked full time. We were making $325 a month as a couple. No insurance, no retirement, there were no benefits of any kind.

Author: What happened if someone got sick or hurt?

Nikki: There were doctors in town (Belen) who would treat the boys free of charge. One young man was run over by a pickup truck and we thought he would never survive (he did). It took the ambulance forty-five minutes to get there. We determined at that point that if we ever had another emergency we would put the child in the car and take them ourselves . . . After several years a roving dental clinic came once a year to clean teeth and repair them. We've always had a bit of a problem with the orthodontic work.

Author: Was food a problem then?

Nikki: We never went without meals, never. I can remember eating noodles until I thought I would gag noodles. One time we had no meat and no money to buy meat, but we had buckets of weenies in the freezer. We had beans and weenies, we had hot dogs, we had barbecued franks. Finally on Saturday the kids came in and said, "What kind of weenies are we having today?"

... One time we had half a truck-load of Oreo cookies donated. It got to be where punishment was eating an Oreo cookie!

Author: What other kinds of jobs did you do?

Nikki: Your job description was, "You work for the Ranch and you do whatever needs to be done." I took some training in what is called The Monterey Reading Program which is a corrective program. I worked with kids on that for about three days a week. Almost all of our kids had problems in school and we began to look for ways to encourage the academics.

... We started an honor roll system and those who had a 2.5 or better would get to fill their plates first when we ate cafeteria style. We also awarded them a trip out to eat or some kind of activity like skating.

... When we opened the new office building there was a library that I helped develop as much as I could. Later, Dorothy King and some of the librarians in town came and cataloged the books.

Author: Did you interview kids?

Nikki: Yes, and helped with the evaluations. Later, I developed forms for us to use in the social work part of it. Today the administrators do that.

Author: Were some of these kids given the choice, either you go to Boys Ranch and straighten yourself out or it's Springer?

Nikki: Oh yes, and that still happens. Parents threaten their kids that way. Juvenile probation officers do that, we have judges that do that. I remember one (judge) sentenced a kid to Boys Ranch and we had to call him back and tell him he couldn't do that. Not all of the kids come from dysfunctional families, but probably the majority of them do.

Author: What prompted an adoption agency?

Nikki: It's an interesting question. We had a little five-year old boy and then the mother asked the Morgans to take the seven-year old daughter. We kept noticing that there were kids that did well for a while, but if they didn't get special attention the problem returned. We were moving kids in and out of our house. We had three boys living with us most of the time. That's really when we wanted to start foster care, where they could have the value of living in a home environment and understand how a family works. We realized that we could probably do adoption and that some of these kids might be able to go ahead and move into an adoptive setting with the family. When we started to have a foster care agency, we realized we could do both at the same time. Everybody had this desire for it to happen and it took a whole lot of effort to get the ball rolling in that direction. Bob Hoberling was the first director. It was a real rough beginning. Our first family was five brothers. We learned a lot of things.

Author: What is something that you would like to share?

Nikki: When we did the fortieth reunion of the Ranch we went through the files (molded at that time due to water in fireproof cabinets). We found that the original files were limited. There were Board meeting minutes, but very little on the kids.

. . . We did determine that probably over two thousand kids have come through the program. And we've cared for a little over 100 girls since we have had the Girls Ranch. Also kids stayed at the Ranch longer in the early days. I think the changes lead to more burnout with houseparents now than it used to. Our average longevity for house parents is about two-and-a-half years and the national average is about six months

. . . We need to help houseparents understand where the kids are coming from. We require that they take a minimum of fourteen hours of training a year. We provide a training program through The New Mexico Christian Child Care Association.

. . . There is never an end to the ministry. But you've got to have a certain amount of self care or you won't survive. Getting people to understand that delicate balance is very difficult.[25]

Story Three: PHIL and MARILYN GREGORY

Phil and Marilyn Gregory both come from Kansas. Both have degrees in education from John Brown University in Arkansas. Phil has a Masters Degree in history from the University of Missouri at Kansas City. It was a teaching-coaching job at the Laguna Indian Reservation that first lured the Gregorys to New Mexico. It was while both Phil and Marilyn were employed by the Belen School System that they first encountered boys from the Ranch. Since both Gregorys were active in the Belen First Baptist Church (where the boys attended), an additional relationship developed with the Ranch. When the Tremblys moved to the Hart Youth Ranch, the Gregorys were selected as the new Boys Ranch administrators.

Author: Exactly when did you and Marilyn come to the Boys Ranch?

Phil: We arrived in August of 1984. I had taught in the Belen schools for eight years and had had a lot of interaction with the Boys Ranch boys.

Author: **What has changed since you first knew of the Boys Ranch?**

Phil: The type of boy! Ten, fifteen years ago they were a western type, chewing tobacco and a tougher type of boy. When I coached at Belen we'd get fertilizer for the track and football field every year and we called it Boys Ranch dip because so many of the boys dipped (tobacco). Those boys were more independent. Today they can't survive at fifteen and sixteen.

Author: **Do you have whole families go through Boys Ranch?**

Phil: We had a set of five brothers that went through the program. The last one graduated two years ago from Hart Ranch. Then I had another five brothers. There's three left in the program. We've had a set of identical twins, which was fun.

. . . This is one of the few places left in the United States that's a working ranch in the real sense of the word. We have 2400 acres and three hundred and some acres that are irrigated. We put up five hundred tons of hay a year. We move the hay from the field to the barns or onto a truck using the small bales o fifty to seventy pounds. The boys work with animals and they take turns with the barn chores. The boys are actually working and riding horses in contact with a ranching situation. These are virtually all town boys and probably forty percent come out of Albuquerque.

Author: **Does a kid come here voluntarily?**

Phil: Yes. Basically, it's a verbal agreement. They give us "loco parentis" authority as long as they are here. We have one boy that's available for adoption, but they never found the right family. We have space for forty-eight and license for fifty. Our average boy is about 12.6 years old. We probably run fifteen applications for every one we can accept . . . We have the same number of houses and houseparents as when I came (eight parents). I did replace the livestock manager with a full-time maintenance man. I used to look for young couples. Today I look for a specific type of personality. They (houseparents) need some real experience with children and kids with difficult backgrounds. Today we spend more money on training than recruitment. The houseparents have to be able to work as we divide up all the jobs on the Ranch.

Author: Marilyn, how do you divide up the boys?

Marilyn: We have twelve boys in each cottage and most houseparents feel reasonably comfortable toward one age group or another. You have to keep it a family-type setting. We have on-going training.

           . . . We started our independent living program because some parents do not want to be involved with their training or their growing. They show it by fewer and fewer letters, phone calls, et cetera. Even when we push them to come to evaluation, they don't.

Author: Can you give a case example?

Marilyn: We had a case where the mother and father were alcoholics. The mother died and the father remarried. The wife and her children and the father lived in the house. The boys lived in a trailer behind the house. The trailer had no heat, water or electricity. The family in the house would eat and the boys got the leftovers. The living situation was absolutely atrocious.

Author: Do the kids who come to the Ranch have learning problems?

Marilyn: Almost ninety percent of the referrals we get, school is a big part of it. Their grades are low. They are frustrated or lack motivation. Our big emphasis, school-wise, is on teaching them study skills. We have quiet time—study time. We talk regularly with their teachers. We try to watch the friends they choose and this is a problem where peer pressure is great.

Author: So you teach them responsibility?

Marilyn: Right. In fact, one of the primary things around here is to be responsible for whatever assignment they are given. Be responsible for it and get it done. You respond better when you feel like you are contributing something and that people are depending on you.

Phil: There's probably about a third of the kids that are referred to us that need residential psychiatric help.

Author: Are you equipped to give that kind of aid?

Phil: No. If we have a boy that comes in our program and he develops needs, we can help him through psychological services. We can do references. We have one boy that terminated from our program after two-and-a-half years. He is now at a psychiatric treatment center.[26]

Story Four: BILL and MARTHA BARRICK

Bill and Martha Barrick are tried and true Texans who met during their high school days in Wichita Falls. For those readers not familiar with that area, it is often called "Tornado Alley" for the large number of storms that go through that part of north Texas. Or as Bill says, "It's the hottest place anywhere in summer and the coldest place in winter, with bad weather most of the time." Bill and Martha married the day after she graduated from high school. In June 1994 these Boys Ranch employees will celebrate their fortieth wedding anniversary. After working a wide variety of jobs, Bill ended up in the aircraft industry building Huey Cobras during the Vietnam War.

Author: How did you get from Texas to the Boys Ranch?

Martha: The music director of our Baptist church in Fort Worth introduced us to Barry Morgan who was looking for houseparents. We came out here in January 1972. Within one hour they put me up on a horse to go down in the fields and find the boys.

Our seven-year old son loved that. At first our older son did not like the move, but he came around and went on to be a member of the National Honor Society, the high school band drum major, and went to the state track meet.

Author: Bill, what did you do when you came to work at the Ranch?

Bill: We were hired as houseparents, but we did most anything. I worked as the maintenance man for a while. Then I worked with the irrigation system. We were houseparents for five years (today they are the cooks) and then I was put in charge of the livestock. We built the barn down bottom, the rodeo arena, and a lot of the wooden corrals.

Author: Let us talk about finances in those years. Things were tight?

Martha: Things were tight. I told Mike and Charles that I didn't think that we could make it because we weren't making ends meet. We didn't have enough money to pay our bills. They looked over our checkbook and realized that we were buying the boys shoelaces, shampoo, fruit, et cetera. So they started giving us an extra ten dollars a month to buy things that the Ranch didn't furnish. We all ate all of our meals in the central kitchen. Sometimes we would all work all night to stuff the envelopes and get the mail out. That's when we were doing our own printing. It was pretty rough. We were all doing double duty, triple duty, doing what we could do to save money and make things work.

Author: **What did a houseparent make in 1972?**

Martha: I remember that they told us that if Bill worked in town and I could be the housemother to these sixteen boys, the Ranch would pay him a hundred dollars a month for weekends. We had all the responsibilities, kitchen, chores, car pools, sports runs, band and it was pretty hard.

Author: **I'm intrigued by the fact that these kids had allowances?**

Martha: That was set up after we came. It was a way of teaching them. The little kids got fifty cents a week, the junior high about a dollar and three dollars for the high school boys. They were supposed to save a little. Today we can have a boy help us in the kitchen up to ten hours a week at a dollar an hour. I can raise him after four or five months to a dollar and a quarter besides his allowance.

Author: **Bill, what changes have you seen in the boys over the years?**

Bill: When we first came here we weren't as particular about who we accepted. We had some pretty rough boys. Some of them were quite good at making trouble. I think it's through God's direction that we have designed our program. One experience tacked on top of the other. We feel like we're doing much better and it's obvious that that's true.

Martha: When we were houseparents we'd get older boys that were real streetwise and we didn't know much about them. Now the houseparents even keep in contact with the parents or guardian. Then we had maybe two parents visit in five

years. Now we have visitors day once a month. There's the
stability of the staff. Our staff has been here a number of
years together, we work together, we communicate.

Bill: Now we have good communication with the school system
            in Belen. We have a tutoring program. In 1974 the veterin-
            arians Dr. Blake and Dr. Griggs were a big help and their
            wives were the first tutors.

Author: Over the years, have you had cases where the boys have
            been rejected in school?

Bill: Yes, definitely, but today Marilyn Gregory is our coordin-
            ator with the school. She is good at explaining things and
            knows all of the teachers.

Martha: We have a good reputation now. I think that people feel
            honored when they are invited out to the Ranch.[27]

Story Five: PATTI WRIGHT

Patti Wright comes from a farm family in Horton, Kansas. For some
ten years she worked as an assistant dental technician while her husband, Mike, managed a chain of roller skating rinks. They found themselves counseling young people through their church and on two different occasions cared for foster children. The Wrights were introduced
to Boys Ranch by the youth minister of their church in Kansas. After
correspondence, an interview and a lot of prayer, the Wrights and their
two boys moved to Boys Ranch in 1986. They currently hold the record
for the longest continuous service as houseparents for Boys Ranch.
What follows are excerpts about the daily life of a houseparent taken
from an interview with Patti Wright by the author's wife during the
summer of 1992.

Question: What was your first impression of Boys Ranch?
Patti: We were picked up at the airport by Tommy Tucker and

Don Hawes, characters in their own selves. They drove us
to the Ranch using all back roads past all the shacks and
junk yards they could find. We were shocked at the terrain
and everything. Then we saw Boys Ranch and we said,
"This is an oasis. This is like a Garden of Eden out in the
desert." It was so beautiful, like a small town with nice
houses, a swimming pool and full-sized gymnasium.

Question: Had you had counseling training?

Patti: Yes, through the church, but not enough. Now we have had
a lot through the Ranch. They gave us three days to move
in and relax. We were silly and stupid enough to jump
right in gung-ho. We had thirteen boys. The youngest was
nine and the oldest was sixteen. So we had a lot of different
needs. We hadn't met any of the parents of the kids and we
needed to work with them. We had to make friends with
them before we could get anywhere. They told us the first
time we came in the house, "Well, you won't last three
months or maybe we'll give you six months at max because
everybody just leaves us." They had had three different
sets of houseparents in five years.

Question: How did your own children (two boys) relate?

Patti: Robbie was in sixth grade and Jeremy was in third grade.
They wanted to make friends right off, so they easily got
into trouble. We allowed them to go through the punishment, as a learning process, right along with whatever
punishment was given those kids. The first year was a real
learning process for all of us. Just when you think you've
adjusted and you get to know the kids, they start to behave
like they did at home. This is where you confront the issue
and start working on the problems.

. . . Many of these kids are angry inside, but they're not
angry at you. You just happen to be there. You have to
stand back emotionally and not let it affect you personally.

If you can't do that, you don't last long as houseparents.

Question: How do you operate this large family?

Patti: The school year is stressful. They get up at five o'clock.
           Breakfast is at five-thirty. The food is brought in from the
           kitchen and in the summer we do our own breakfast. Our
           boys are on the bus at six forty-five. Before they can even
           come to the breakfast table they have to clean their room
           and the bathroom. We check their rooms daily. This teaches
           them to be responsible for their own area. There's four of
           them per bathroom. They come to the table dressed and
           ready for school, hair combed, room vacuumed and dust-
           ed, and sink and mirrors clean. We have a devotion time
           before we eat breakfast. We even have an incentive at the
           table. Whoever has the cleanest room the week before gets
           food first. Everything is set up on incentives. After break-
           fast they complete their house job which means the whole
           house is completely cleaned before they go to school. Every
           day it's vacuumed, dusted, swept, all the entries are swept,
           everything is done before they get on the bus.

           . . . During the school year they don't take care of the ani-
           mals in the morning. Mike is the livestock manager and I
           do the paperwork. We have staff meetings and other
           responsibilities.

Question: How do you manage all of the laundry?

Patti: The boys take the clothes over to the laundry and sort it into
           piles so that it is done properly. Put it in the wrong pile and
           it may come back the wrong color. Everything is initialed.
           Before a new boy can put any of their clothes away, we sit
           down on the bed and I help them to initial all of their
           clothes. That's how I get to know them. They do the laun-
           dry once a week. Now we use net bags so they don't have
           to sort everything.

. . . When they come home from school it's snack time and we sit around the table for a few minutes and talk to them about school that day. The boys usually race home to tell us, you know, what has happened. They crave the attention. You spend the rest of your time from the time they come home hearing "Mom this," Mom," "Mom," "Mom," because they want attention. They want to tell you everything that's going on.

. . . They change into chore clothes. Part stay with me and part go with Mike in the back of the truck to do chores. We have calves, lambs, pigs, chickens, cattle, and horses.

. . . Most of our kids are teenagers. Last summer we had one sixth grader who was big for his size and a really bad bully before he came here. He needed to be put into a house with older boys to help him realize he needed to mature.

. . . Friday night is movie night if everything has gone all right at school. Each teacher signs a progress report every week and they have to do their homework every night

. . . Saturday morning we have a big breakfast in the cafeteria. The ones with good grades (2.6 or above) go first. They clean the house and go outside to work for about an hour or hour-and-a-half. You have to inspect everything because these boys are such con artists.

Question: Let's talk about summertime.

Patti: Summer is more relaxed. We get up at seven-thirty and they can stay up until ten o'clock. They can get their own breakfast and I help them to learn to cook. Sunday night is "Cook's Night off." The boys can cook, use the microwave, have leftovers, or eat peanut butter and jelly. We have lazy boys who won't do anything but peanut butter, but most get pulled into cooking. We have had seven-year-olds win contests on omelets. In the summer they do more work with the animals. Our boys all have 4-H projects to work

on. They work hard and they play hard. We have bikes,
basketball, swimming, horses. Summertime is when we do
more horseback riding. In the wintertime the school activities keep them too busy. We like to do a lot of hiking up
in the mountains and spend the day. Take a picnic lunch
and bring back all kinds of souvenirs.

Question: It really is a family, isn't it?

Patti: I don't always have good days and the boys know that.
           They sense it and they jump right in to do things. They
           really care for you. When they're sick, we really pamper
           them . . . We're required to take them to church every
           Sunday. But we also have neat devotional times with the
           boys—they're anxious to learn.

Question: How do you deal with letting go?

Patti: That's the hardest lesson that any houseparent ever has to
           learn at the Ranch. They're a part of your family and a part
           of you goes with them wherever they go. You have to learn
           to let go and put them in God's hands. So you say a little
           prayer and send them off on their way, and wait. There's
           very few that haven't contacted us. One boy calls regular
           and says, "You know I'll never let you down."[28]

Story Six: BERT and BRENDA SCHRADER

Bert and Brenda Schrader, the administrators at Girls Ranch, were
both born and raised in Corpus Christi, Texas where they attended the
same church.

Bert did a three-year stint in the U.S. Army, including eighteen
months in Vietnam with a helicopter outfit. Bert graduated from Texas
A&I in 1972 with a degree in business management. Five years later he
completed his Masters Degree in public administration from North
Texas State University. During the years that Bert worked for Dallas

County, one of his more interesting assignments was to collect information concerning the Texas Schoolbook Depository Building from which President John F. Kennedy was assassinated.

Brenda married Bert when she was eighteen, with one year of college behind her. Later, she became an orthodontic assistant and continued working part time after they started taking in foster children. A few years later, she started her own business of tracing x-rays and grinding models for orthodontists. Brenda is in charge of all the social work at Girls Ranch.

Author: How did you end up at Girls Ranch?

Bert: Partly because I had worked at the Mount Lebanon Baptist Encampment, which is the third largest in the U.S. right after Glorieta and Ridgecrest. Brenda and I felt a call into this kind of ministry. We applied through InterChristo and got a letter from Charles Gibson. When I read his letter, I knew instantly that this was the place I should be. Brenda and I came as a couple. We are co-administrators and do things together here at the Ranch.

Author: Brenda, what did a girl from Texas think of this place the first time you saw it?

Brenda: I'm not crazy about deserts. I'm from Corpus Christi with lots of humidity and beautiful grass. I wasn't anxious to leave Texas. After we met Sandy and Phil Lutz, we met some of the girls and I just absolutely fell in love (with them). There were fourteen girls here then (1987).

Bert: Girls Ranch was in a seven-year plan. We now have twenty girls. Our dining room was built in '87; a swimming pool was built in '91; the tennis courts were built in '90. Barns and other things have been added. We have completed a master plan for Girls Ranch and that plan calls for one more dorm to be built for another ten girls. Girls Ranch capacity at its peak would be thirty. Maybe thirty-five if we added an independent living place on campus.

Author: **What's unique about a Girls Ranch?**

Brenda: We look at each girl and try to figure out what each girl needs in their life. A lot of them need extra help in counseling. They need love, that's the big thing, and they need Christ in their lives.

Bert: Normally, upwards of 90% of our girls are sexually abused. We have good girls from bad situations. Normally, the scenario is that it's a dysfunctional family who really can't provide for the child. In most cases they are a single parent family. The youngest I have now is twelve and the oldest is nineteen. Our average (age) is about fourteen-and-a-half, right now.

Author: **Do any of these girls ever run away?**

Brenda: Some go walk around a while and think about it. Before we came there was a girl that actually got in with a trucker and took off with him.

Bert: We haven't had any runaways in years, but right after Brenda and I came here we had a couple of girls who went to the train station (just over the hill from the Ranch is Lamy which is an AMTRAK stop) and we went down and found them. Perhaps if there had been a train there they might have tried.

Author: **Are these tough girls?**

Brenda: Some of them are really tough. And some of them are too tough for us to handle because we aren't a treatment center. I look to see if the girl really has a desire to change and sometimes it's "iffy."

Bert: Normally it's an eighteen-month stay and it's voluntary, which is very unusual. I think it's great because a girl must sit down and do an interview. We like for her to verbalize that they want to go through a change . . . They carry a lot of guilt with them.

Author: **Do they all go to the same school?**

Bert: We go to seven different schools because our girls normally come to us behind academically. (Today there is an on-campus school.) We work real diligently to maintain a good relationship, good rapport with our schools and with our teachers. I think that eight of our girls are seeing the same counselor. She is a real, real good counselor and is starting to push some buttons to get to the root cause of some problems.

Author: **Do the girls show a certain affection for the animals at the Ranch?**

Bert: It's a good way to let them have some responsibility and express some love to a thing that will not come down on them. The animal is not going to think badly of them even when they fail. We have ten pigs, fourteen horses, three steers, two lambs, some rabbits, peacocks, a variety of dogs and cats. All the girls are pretty active in at least dealing with some animal. We have our own 4-H chapter here.

Author: **Have any of the girls gone on to college?**

Brenda: Yes, Sharon Brown, the first girl to graduate from Girls Ranch is teaching now. Katie Luck won every award imaginable and got a full basketball scholarship to Western New Mexico State University.

Author: **What is your biggest headache as an administrator?**

Brenda: Having ten people that can mesh together and work together on a twenty-four hour stressful day.

Bert: You know, I equate that to a small city and you have people problems. The biggest concerns are insuring that our girls feel loved and secure, that they can leave here feeling nurtured and having come to know the Lord as their Savior. You live in very, very close proximity. You work in an environment which is sometimes highly charged and you constantly deal with people's emotions.

        . . . The one thing that I like for people to understand about Girls Ranch in particular, but also about Boys Ranch, is that we create a family environment, a family environment not unlike a large family that you would see most anywhere. I'd just like for people to know that Girls Ranch is here because a lot of people are interested in what we do and because they love kids.[29]

Story Seven: RICHARD B. GREGORY

     Chairman of the Board of Directors, "Rich" Gregory was born on December 12, 1944 in Ludlow, Massachusetts. His father was a career Air Force man and like all military families, the Gregorys moved on a regular basis. High school graduation found "Rich" at Burns Flat, Oklahoma, while his father was stationed at the nearby Clinton Sherman Air Base. Gregory graduated from college at Texas Tech, took an MBA from Eastern New Mexico and received his law degree from the University of New Mexico. Gregory now lives and practices law in Las Cruces, New Mexico.

Author: How did you get interested in the Boys Ranch?

Rich: Well, I was pretty involved with the Presbyterian Church and was even on the Board of the Menaul School in Albuquerque. As a tax lawyer I was involved with a lot of charitable things. I got involved with the Boys Ranch through my connection with Ted Bonnell and Bank Securities, Inc. He was Chairman of the Board (Boys Ranch & BSI) and he asked me to do some deferred giving documents for the Boys Ranch because they didn't have an active development program at the time.

Author: When did you come on the Board and in what capacity?

Rich: Probably '82 or '83 because they had formed a committee to look into starting Girls Ranch and Alice King asked me to serve on that committee.

Author: Would you explain the difference between the Board of Advisors and the Board of Directors?

Rich: The Board of Directors has the management responsibility, the overall operation of the Boys Ranch as an entity. The Board of Advisors is a group of people who don't have the same legal responsibility and yet have a feeling for the organization and a desire to help. All Directors must first serve on the Board of Advisors.

Author: Is there a specific number on each board?

Rich: No, there isn't even a limit to the number of advisors. There are about twenty-five. There are more advisors than directors. Now that we have the Foundation, we will have a Board of Directors for that as well. The Board elects new members, so it's a self-perpetuating board. We have a nominating committee and then an election at the Annual Meeting in February each year.

Author: Let's talk about the composition of the Board. Is there any attempt made to balance it? Male, female, religiously, ethnically, or in any way?

Rich: In the past there wasn't much thought to that. It was finding people who would volunteer to work long hours for no pay. We've traditionally had more Baptists than others, but a belief in Jesus Christ as your Lord and Savior is the only criteria, so we have all kinds, even Presbyterians like me. More importantly, we have been trying very hard to get particular skills on the Board. We need people with experience in finances, for example accountants. We have a strong identity with the ranchers and farmers, so we need people in that sector. We need people with big-time management skills like corporations. It's an economic thing . . .

We have just added Dr. Gerald May to the Board of Advisors (now a full Board member). Dr. May was the immediate past President of the University of New Mexico.

Author: Is geographical distribution important?

Rich: Geographics are important also. We have had a very strong identity with Bernallio County, Albuquerque, and Belen. We are trying very hard to move away from that. One of the good things about me moving to Las Cruces was that people are starting to say, "You know, Boys Ranch is here, too." We are doing better than we did ten years ago.

Author: Does the size of the state make Board meetings difficult?

Rich: It's very difficult when you have to drive two hundred and ninety miles to a meeting. J.B. Tidwell is the prime example. He has a three hundred and ten mile drive if we meet in Albuquerque, each way. It's not going to get any better. We occasionally do telephone conferences for important things that are of short notice. We are going to have to live with it. We have rotated our Board meetings, over the years, to go to each of the facilities. We're going to continue to do that so that it's part of the indoctrination, education process for the Board members.

Author: The Ranch has such a strong religious philosophy as to what it does and how it's done, and yet there has never been a chaplain at any of the facilities. Is every dorm parent viewed as a chaplain?

Rich: It's a priesthood of all believers type of philosophy. The houseparents are responsible, the administrators are responsible, and some of the kids are responsible. You know we don't require the kids to be Christians. That's not part of the criteria. We do quite a bit of training. The Southwest Association of Homes for Children do a number of programs. We try very hard to equip them (houseparents). That is one of the tenets of the fiftieth year plan. It's a tough situation. You know, houseparents burn out very quickly. We have a much longer term for most of our houseparents than the national average.

Author: What is next?

Rich: We've been trying to get ourselves on a sound fiscal basis. We would like to help a lot more kids. We'd like to help families. "Families" is the key word in our fiftieth year plan. We're going to go very slowly and we're not going to jeopardize this entire organization for one great idea. We recognize that we are in the business of helping kids. And helping kids doesn't necessarily mean residential care. I think that we will find that we're getting more and more into preventive ministry.[30]

Story Eight: MICHAEL H. KULL

Michael H. Kull, President of New Mexico Boys and Girls Ranch, was born in El Paso, Texas in 1946. His father was a native New Mexican and his grandfather had homesteaded in southern New Mexico in the late 1800s. Abandoned by their father when Mike was twelve years old, the five Kull children ended up being raised at the Baptist Children's Home in Portales.

Author: How did you learn about the Boys Ranch?

Mike: Well, as you know, Walker Hubbard was the superintendent of the Baptist Children's Home and simultaneously
was the superintendent of the Boys Ranch. He had the reputation of the premier child care expert in the state of New
Mexico. Between 1954 and 1972 he divided his time between the two facilities. I credit him with saving the Ranch.

Author: So you knew Hubbard at the Children's Home?

Mike: That's correct. When I was in high school, Mr. Hubbard
allowed the older kids to chauffeur him because he drove
back and forth so much. In fact, he would buy a new car
about every eighteen months, and his old car would always
have in excess of a hundred thousand miles on it. He loved
big wildcat Buicks.

Author: What would you do at Boys Ranch?

Mike: I would just roam around with the kids or mess with the
animals. There was always something to do. This was in
the early sixties.

. . . 1968 was the year that the last payment was made on
the debt. Everything went to pay off that debt. The Board
then sat down and developed a ten-year plan. So the first
cottage had already been completed and the second cottage
was under construction when I came to the Ranch in 1970.
We have a joke in our family that the day we came to the
Ranch, Nikki cried all day. It looked very desolate, very
few trees, no paved roads. One of the jokes was that everyone had a telephone, but they were all five and six-party
lines. Therewas no such thing as a private conversation.

Author: Who was in charge of the Ranch?

Mike: Barry Morgan! Let me explain the connection. When I was a senior in high school at the Children's Home, Barry Morgan and his wife became my houseparents. After I left the Children's Home, Barry and Martha came to the Boys Ranch. I remember thinking that this is a real ranch—horses, cattle. In the early days there were lots of kids and very little supervision. It was a shoestring operation.

. . . I think that one of the advantages the Ranch has always had is the real estate. The ability to roam. Plenty of work, crops, cattle, hogs, just a Huck Finn attitude. Plenty of room to roam, to look for arrowheads and rocks and frogs and the things that boys like to do.

Author: Were these boys juvenile delinquents?

Mike: Many of them were in the early years. They weren't sentenced there, but it was an "us against the world" attitude. Before Barry the kids all dressed alike. They all wore the same kind of jackets. That identification factor kind of made a gang atmosphere. We worked hard to change that atmosphere. To have transportation for every cottage where they would not have to go in large groups.

. . . Many of the kids would tell us, "This is the first time in my life I've ever had enough to eat." On one occasion we took them to a Mexican buffet restaurant. The guy told me, "I'll make you a five-hundred dollar a year contribution to your Ranch if you won't ever bring those kids back!" One boy ate the complete buffet and then ate twenty-four tacos and still wanted more.

Author: The kids that come here come from all kinds of diverse backgrounds. How do you address their specific needs?

Mike: The early kids just showed up and we accepted them. In their file there might be one page. It's been probably a combination of the government regulations increasing and more resource becoming available. Shot records became important, school records became important. When we came in 1970 there was not a standardized system. We set all of that up later. Much of what exists today was developed in conjunction with the National Association of Homes for Children in trying to develop national standards for that kind of thing. We do complete progress evaluations on the kids every six months. That started in about 1980.

Author: What has changed the most in the years you have been associated with the Ranch?

Mike: We went from being a one, homogenous, small, single focus child care facility to a multi-faceted corporation with five different locations. Included are adoption, infant adoption, foster care, and three residential programs. There's a greater emphasis now on after care and in working with the families of the kids. Our next major thrust is doing more for families, so that when these kids get ready to go home that the family has changed too.

. . . When I came to the Ranch there was a lot of bickering among the staff members. It really distressed me a lot. One of the first things that I did when I became superintendent in '72 was to get the Board to change the charter of the Ranch into a Christian organization. I think that was a turning point in the Ranch. The definition is very broad, but one thing that is important is your attitude toward Jesus Christ. Doctrinal things are not important. I think that is one of the reasons that God has blessed our organization so much. We've developed a very unique way of allowing the kids to know what is important without beating them over the head. I think we have to get back to a greater tolerance of each others' differences.

Author: Where does the money come from?

Mike: You ought to read the letters. Right now we have 28,000 people (donors) scattered all over the United States. Last count I took, about 28% of them were from out of state. A lot of government and military people maintain the contact. We have some very large donors, usually around Christmas. We found out that we have one of the highest donor loyalty rates in the United States. It puts a real responsibility on us.

Author: Has your budget steadily gone up?

Mike: Oh yeah! The first budget I remember was in 1970 for a little over $87,000 and in 1992 it's almost two million. Now we have five locations and take care of one hundred sixty kids a year.

Author: What's your vision of the future?

Mike: We've just come through a stage of expansion, more kids, more facilities, doing more to help kids. Now, for the next few years, we are going to go into doing a more effective job with what you have. In other words, improving the quality of life of the kids. Start turning out kids who are better equipped to deal with the complex culture which they are going into and be better able to succeed in that environment. My vision is to diversify more and the other is, while we diversify to keep that quality high.[31]

NOTES:

1. The Corral NMBR Newsletter, Winter 1990.
2. Ibid.
3. Ibid.
4. Ibid.
5. Ibid.
6. The Corral NMBR Newsletter, Winter 1991.
7. Ibid.
8. The Corral NMBR Newsletter, Summer 1991.
9. The Corral NMBR Newsletter, Fall 1991.

10. The Corral NMBR Newsletter, Spring 1992.
11. Ibid.
12. Various conversations—correspondence from Mike Kull, 1993-1994.
13. Unpublished document NMBR, 1993.
14. The Corral NMBR Newsletter, Fall 1993.
15. The Corral NMBR Newsletter, Winter 1994.
16. Ibid.
17. Ibid.
18. The Interpreter's Dictionary of the Bible, Abingdon Press, Nashville: TN, 1962, pp. 1001-1002.
19. The Layman's Bible Commentary, John Knox Press, Richmond: VA, 1963, p. 67.
20. The Corral, New Mexico Boys and Girls Ranch, Fall 1993.
21. Interview with Michael H. Kull, May 28, 1992, Albuquerque, New Mexico.
22. Ibid.
23. Ibid.
24. Interview with J.B. Tidwell, June 17, 1991, Hobbs, New Mexico.
25. Interview with Nikki Kull, May 27, 1992, Albuquerque, New Mexico.
26. Interview with Phil and Marilyn Gregory, July 8, 1990, Boys Ranch, New Mexico.
27. Interview with Bill and Martha Barrick, June 24, 1991, Boys Ranch, New Mexico.
28. Interview with Patti Wright by Shirley Terry, June 3, 1992, Boys Ranch, New Mexico.
29. Interview with Bert and Brenda Schrader, June 10, 1992, Girls Ranch, New Mexico.
30. Interview with Richard B. Gregory, June 19, 1991, Las Cruces, New Mexico.
31. Interview with Michael H. Kull, May 28, 1992, Albuquerque, New Mexico.

EPILOGUE

The story of the New Mexico Boys Ranch is one of unbelievable sacrifice. Only God knows the human drama that has transpired here. The thread common to all has been its ability to permanently change the lives of everyone whom it touches or who touched it.

Many became involved because they wanted to make a difference by helping children and giving them a better life, but soon realized they had been forever changed themselves in ways they did not realize were possible. A characteristic of God is to work in our lives in ways we least suspect, and he has done so here in marvelous ways.

I know many who have made tremendous sacrifices who are not mentioned in these pages, and God knows many more. It is a tribute to the wonderful people of New Mexico who are always ready to lend a helping hand with little thought of themselves.

We do not believe He has brought us this far without a purpose. There is much left to do and we are confident the New Mexico Boys Ranch is an instrument God will continue to use for His purpose if we will but commit it to Him. This is also true of those who have faithfully supported and labored in this work year after year without thought of personal acclaim. We are confident there is One who will never forget their sacrifice.

Michael H. Kull
President
Albuquerque, New Mexico

BIBLIOGRAPHY

In order to fully grasp the significance of the story of The New Mexico Boys Ranch it is necessary to appreciate the land, the history, and the culture of New Mexico. The following books have proven to be valuable for that purpose.

Beck, Warren A. and Ynez D. Haase. *Historical Atlas of New Mexico.* University of Oklahoma Press, 1979.
Biebel, Charles D. *Making the Most of It: Public Works in Albuquerque During The Great Depression: 1929 – 1942.* Albuquerque, The Museum of Albuquerque, 1986.
Chavez, Fray Angelico. *My Penitent Land: Reflections on Spanish New Mexico.* Albuquerque, New Mexico: University of New Mexico Press, 1974.
Gjeure, John A. *Chile Line: The Narrow Rail Trail to Santa Fe.* Espanola, N.M. Rio Grande Sun Press, 1984.
Hillerman, Tony. *The Spell of New Mexico.* Albuquerque, New Mexico: University of New Mexico Press, 1976.
New Mexico In Maps. Edited by Jerry L. Williams and Paul E. McAllister. Albuquerque, University of New Mexico, 1979.
New Mexico Place Names: A Geographical Dictionary. ed. T.M. Pearce. University of New Mexico Press, 1965.
Ortiz, Alfonso. *Red Power On The Rio Grande.* Chicago: Follet Publishing Co., 1973.
Simmons, Marc. *Albuquerque: A Narrative History.* University of New Mexico Press, 1983.
Simmons, Marc. *Coronado's Land: Essays on Daily Life In Colonial New Mexico.* Albuquerque, University of New Mexico Press, 1991.
Simmons, Marc. *New Mexico: A History.* W.W. Norton and Company, Inc., 1977.
Simmons, Marc. *The Last Conquistador.* Norman, Oklahoma. University of Oklahoma Press, 1991.
Sinclair, John. *New Mexico: The Shining Land.* University of New Mexico, 1980.
Walker, Randi Jones. *Protestantism In the Sangre de Cristos.* University of New Mexico Press, 1963.
Weber, David J. *New Spain's Far Northern Frontier.* Albuquerque, University of New Mexico Press, 1979.

ORAL HISTORY INTERVIEWS

Barber, Richard/Jeanette	Las Cruces, New Mexico	June 19, 1991
Barnes, B.G.	Albuquerque, New Mexico	June 22, 1991
Barricks, William/Martha	Boys Ranch, New Mexico	June 24, 1991
Blevins Family	Clovis, New Mexico	June 16, 1991
Britton, Wayne	Ft. Worth, Texas	May 20, 1992
Cantwell, Oscar	Clovis, New Mexico	June 15, 1991
Cole, Regina	Belen, New Mexico	May 25, 1992
Gibson, Charles	Boys Ranch, New Mexico	May 24, 1992
Gibson, Margaret	Boys Ranch, New Mexico	May 31, 1992
Gonzales, Tony	Boys Ranch, New Mexico	May 31, 1992
Gregory, Marilyn	Boys Ranch, New Mexico	August 8, 1990
Gregory, Phillip	Boys Ranch, New Mexico	August 8, 1990
Gregory, Richard	Las Cruces, New Mexico	June 19, 1991
Holder, Billie	Alamogordo, New Mexico	June 18, 1991
Holmbach, John	Grand Junction, Colorado	June 20, 1992
Houston, Dwight	Hurley, New Mexico	June 20, 1991
Hubbard, Dorothy	Belen, New Mexico	June 24, 1991
Kull, Michael	Albuquerque, New Mexico	May 27, 1992
Kull, Nikki	Albuquerque, New Mexico	May 28, 1992
Lowrance, Gerry	Belen, New Mexico	May 25, 1992
May, Jesse	Farmington, New Mexico	June 8, 1992
Morgan, Barr	Ft. Worth, Texas	May 20, 1992
Ratliff, Jack	Albuquerque, New Mexico	June 25, 1991
Schrader, Bert/Brenda	Girls Ranch, Lamy, New Mexico	June 10, 1992
Stagg, Harry	Albuquerque, New Mexico	June 27, 1991
Tidwell, J.B.	Hobbs, New Mexico	June 17, 1991
Torres, Mela	Boys Ranch, New Mexico	June 4, 1992
Trembly, Mozelle	Roswell, New Mexico	June 1, 1992
Tucker, Tommy	Boys Ranch, New Mexico	May 24, 1992
Ulibarri, Escquil	Vequita, New Mexico	May 25, 1992
Underwood, Dub	Albuquerque, New Mexico	June 26, 1991
Waid, Carter	Belen, New Mexico	June 24, 1991
Wright, Patti	Boys Ranch, New Mexico	June 3, 1992

INDEX

THE AUTHOR

Dr. Robert H. Terry, a native Pennsylvanian, is a Full Professor at York College of Pennsylvania and director of its Oral History Center. He is an active member of Calvary United Methodist Church in Dillsburg where he serves as Lay Leader. He is a Lay Speaker in the United Methodist Church, a delegate to Annual Conference and a member of the Board of Directors of the Neighborhood Center in Harrisburg, Pennsylvania.

Dr. Terry is the author of a number of books and monographs including: *Light In The Valley: The McCurdy Mission School Story* (Sunstone 1984), and *Neighborhood Center: An Urban Love Story* (Mennonite 1992).